BREAKING THE CHAINS
Understanding Religious Addiction and Religious Abuse

Breaking the Chains

by Father Leo Booth

Understanding RELIGIOUS ADDICTION and RELIGIOUS ABUSE

Emmaus Publications
195 Claremont Avenue
Suite 388
Long Beach, CA 90803
(213) 434-4813

DEDICATION

To all those who have suffered in the name of God and by the name of God. May they discover the TRUTH that ultimately sets all people free.

TABLE of CONTENTS

OUTLINE

PART ONE: The Problem

Chapter 1: Background -

Defining religious addiction as compulsive behavior.

Relationship between religious addiction and family dysfunction.

Role religious addiction/abuse plays in TV evangelism.

TV evangelist scandal.

Cross-addiction and its relationship with religious addiction.

Relapse issues.

Chapter 2: Dysfunctional Behavior

Examine the problem of religious addiction.

A comparison between the effects of religious addiction and alcoholism.

A diagram chart showing the progression of religious addiction in three stages:
A. Early stage
B. Middle stage
C. Late stage

The effects of religious addiction on the whole person.

List of 20 symptoms with detailed description.

Chapter 3: The Co-dependent

The effects of religious addiction on the spouse.

Tracing the dysfunction in husband and wife: similar to *Women Who Love Too Much.* Conspiracy of silence.

Chapter 4: Adult Children Issues

Serious effects on the children: As with children of alcoholics, we see the following roles:
A) Hero
B) Scapegoat
C) Lost Child
D) Family Mascot

Characteristics of Adult Child.

Explanation of guilt and shame issues.

Chapter 5: Who Is at Risk?

Those who have chemical dependency problems - or have compulsive behavior problems (i.e. overeaters, workaholics, perfectionists).

Those with low self-esteem.

The sexually/physically/emotionally abused.

Children from religiously addicted parents.

The elderly.

The sick.

Teenagers: desires for serenity,
black and white answers,
gain power and authority.

Chapter 6: Personal Stories

A religious addict who grew up in a religiously addictive home.

A child who came from an alcoholic parent who escaped into religion.

An abused child who became a religious addict because of the non-physical love of Jesus (also an over-eater).

A mother who became compulsive over a TV ministry because of a sick child (leukemia).

Homosexual: thought Jesus would take away his perverted feelings.

Old woman: lonely, depressed, afraid of dying (husband died year earlier).

Story of parents who lost a child to a Christian religious group...child became fanatical and rejected them.

An insecure perfectionist woman who became a religious addict - by marrying a religious addict (who physically abused her).

Part Two: The Solution

Chapter 7: Intervention

Pre-intervention meeting (1) Explaining the disease and how it affects the family, friends. What they need to do - write incidences and relevant information.

Pre-intervention meeting (2) Read material family and friends have written. Re-emphasize coming from a place of love. Explain healing process and family's need to be involved in treatment.

Intervention (3) Explain that no intervention really fails - even if the person does not seek help after the "loving encounter." Many may get help later as a result of the intervention.

Chapter 8: Treatment

Detailed explanation of treatment model for religious addiction that fits a chemical dependency treatment center.

Outline of necessary material for treating religious addiction and religious abuse.

Emphasis on family program.

How to form a self-help group based on Twelve Steps of Alcoholics Anonymous.

Chapter 9: Recovery

Explanation of *how to love yourself spiritually.*

Discuss discovering God in your life.

Permission to think, doubt, ask questions.

Develop "God values" (spirituality) in our personal lives.

"For many years I have been concerned about compulsive behavior patterns that affect the alcoholic and drug addict, especially highlighting food addiction, sexual compulsion and co-dependency. Since the recent scandals that have concerned the Bakkers, Oral Roberts and Jimmy Swaggart, and my personal experience with patients who have shared painful experiences concerning religious dysfunction and the numerous addiction conferences that have produced a positive response from the participants to the need for more information concerning religious addiction and religious abuse, it seemed appropriate to concentrate on this neglected 'addiction' and explain treatment techniques and recovery (based upon the 12-step principles)."

Fr. Leo Booth

ACKNOWLEDGEMENT

I wish to thank Cheryl Hirsch, my publicity agent, not only for planting the seed for this book on religious addiction and religious abuse but for her continued encouragement.

Paul Melanson was tireless in his editing, typing and researching historical documentation that made the topic, "religious addiction," come alive. His insights as a substance abuse counselor enabled him to contribute helpful comments and criticisms. Also, thanks to Dane Walker and Cheri Cross. Their hard work, support and expertise helped this book become a reality.

INTRODUCTION

This book is about freedom; religious freedom.

For many years I have been concerned about religious addiction and religious abuse. The recent scandals concerning Jimmy Swaggart and Jim and Tammy Bakker, coupled with the outrageous statements of Oral Roberts and other TV evangelists and the tragedy that I have observed in the "religious" lives of hundreds of alcoholics and drug addicts, have made the writing of this book imperative.

As an Episcopal priest who, for many years, has been working nationally and internationally in developing treatment and recovery techniques for addictive behavior and diagnosing the effect chemical addiction has upon the family, relationships and society, it became apparent to me that, in not a few cases, the addict's religious beliefs were equally dysfunctional. I am not just speaking about members of "fringe" religious denominations and cults, but also those who attend the mainline religious denominations: The compulsive and obsessive behavior that abuses and craves alcohol, cocaine, creates dysfunctional relationships (co-dependency), and also twists and corrupts religious beliefs and practices.

It is important to emphasize and make a distinction between a balanced and healthy religious belief system and that of the obsessive and compulsive religious addict. It is not the intention of this book to suggest that all religions are breeding grounds for addiction or that the majority of religious believers, whether Christian, Jewish, Muslim or "whatever" are addicts or have been religiously abused. However, one of the less known and most widespread symptoms of compulsive behavior and dysfunctional relationships (co-dependency) in our society is its effect upon our use and abuse of religion. Many more people are affected than at first would seem apparent. Indeed, religious addiction as a distinct aspect of compulsive and obsessive behavior, separate from drug abuse, is widespread in our culture.

It is my belief that religious addiction can be described as a disease, a compulsive dysfunctional behavior that is similar to other addictions: alcoholism, co-dependency, workaholism, eating disorders and obsessions concerning sex and gambling. The religious addict uses God, the Bible or a TV evangelist to "fix" his/ her life and magically remove the problems, making it appear better, more meaningful and happy. As with the other addictions, religious addiction/abuse is rooted and thrives in low self-esteem, guilt, feelings of isolation and "difference."

We live in an addictive society. We are compulsive around alcohol, food, drugs, sex, gambling, TV, people, work, physical exercise - the list seems endless. Why should we be surprised to discover that compulsive or addictive behavior or abuse can be exhibited where God, the Bible and religion are concerned?

As with other addictive, compulsive behaviors, the family and relationships are affected. The religious addict creates a family dysfunction and abuses the people he loves (and who love him). Just as millions of people are getting in touch with the physical and emotional pain of growing up as children with an alcoholic parent, so I believe that millions of people have been affected by growing up in a home where a parent (or parents and grandparents) suffered from the disease of religious addiction. The guilt, fear and shame created by a judgmental and vengeful God continue to create dysfunctional lives - and the sickness is passed on.

However, this book brings hope. Just as there has been healing and recovery in the lives of the alcoholic community, so with similar insights, understanding, acceptance and treatment we can bring healing and recovery to those who are religiously addicted or abused. The alcoholic requires an honest and accepting "spiritual program"; this also is true for the religious addict. God is not a prisoner of any one religion or denomination. God is to be found in the freedom of His/Her creation. Spirituality is finding God in a loving lifestyle, not in dogma.

Many will be angered and shocked by this book, others will be disturbed and confused. This is to be expected. Not a few will feel relieved and affirmed by what they read. But I don't think that anybody will be in any doubt that religious addiction and abuse exists; it has symptoms and characteristics - and it can be treated.

Are you a religious addict? Have you been religiously abused? Take a deep breath and read on!

Chapter 1

BACKGROUND

Addiction. We cannot escape it. Everywhere we turn, we are confronted on television and radio, in magazines and in local newspapers with the war on drugs, the cocaine epidemic and the problem of substance abuse. Facts and statistics concerning teen-agers being hooked on "crack" and the astronomical profits made from the sale of drugs are commonplace. The waste and devastation that drugs cause to industry and commerce, the thousands of senior citizens playing one doctor against another in order to obtain prescription drugs, the innocent babies being born addicted because of their mother's drug habit - all have been researched and documented. In response to this "drug war," the Reagan government mounted a colossal education and propaganda campaign - "Say No to Drugs" - reminding us that drugs are society's number one enemy! We are all involved.

Intermingled with drug abuse are obsessions around food, sex, work, shopping (credit-cards) and gambling. There are so many aspects to addiction that it is not an exaggeration to say we have become an addicted society.

In her book, *When Society Becomes An Addict,* Ann Wilson Schaef states:

Much of what we know about our society can be compared to what the blind persons knew about the elephant. As that old story teaches us, an elephant is more than just ears, a tail or a trunk; it is more, even, than just an animal. It is also a process within a context. It is born, it lives, and it dies. This is a process.

BREAKING THE CHAINS

The context of our elephant story - our society - is the fact that the system in which we live is an addictive one. It has all the characteristics and exhibits all the processes of the individual alcoholic or addict. It functions in precisely the same ways. To say the society is an addictive system is not to condemn the society, just as an intervention with an alcoholic does not condemn the alcoholic. In fact, those of us who work with addicts know that the most caring thing to do is not to embrace the denial but to confront the disease. This is the only possibility the addict has to recover. Just as with the addict, one has to say that the society has a disease. If it admits having the disease, it has the option of recovery.[1]

Additionally, she writes:

In order to perceive the Addictive System for what it is, one must be in it but not of it. In other words, one must be recovering from its effects. There are people who fit this criterion. Historically, however, the main curing agent for addictions has been anonymous - Alcoholics Anonymous, Al-Anon, Overeaters Anonymous, Gamblers Anonymous and so on. As a result, the people who have the most accurate perceptions of our system have often hidden this knowledge in anonymity.[2]

Other books inform us about how people can become addicted around people: Co-dependency. In *Women Who Love Too Much,* we read:

Addiction is a frightening word. It conjures up images of heroin users jabbing into their arms and leading obviously destructive lives. We don't like the word and we don't want to apply the concept to the way we relate to men. But many, many of us have been "man junkies" and, like any other addict, we need to admit the severity of our problem before we can begin to recover from it.[3]

In *Is It Love or Is It Addiction?* we read:

My experience of love addiction is that it is a reliance on someone external to the self in an attempt to get unmet needs fulfilled, avoid fear or emotional pain, solve problems, and maintain balance. The paradox is that love addiction is an attempt to gain control of our lives, and in so doing, we go out of control by giving personal power to someone other than the self. It is our unhealthy dependency on others. It is very often associated with feelings of "never being enough." Love addiction is also a form of passivity in that we do not directly resolve our problems but attempt to collude with others so they will take care of our problem. We willingly take care of others at our own expense.[4]

A pioneer book, *Adult Children of Alcoholics,* deals with the effects that alcoholism (drugs) has on the children who grew up in a home where alcohol was abused:

There is little question that there are large numbers of children affected by living in alcoholic homes. Identification of these children has been difficult for several reasons including embarrassment, ignorance of alcoholism as a disease, denial, and protection of children from unpleasant realities.

Although the suffering manifests itself behaviorally in different ways, children of alcoholics seem to have in common a low self-esteem. This is not surprising, since the literature indicates that the conditions which lead an individual to value himself as a person of worth can be briefly summarized by the terms "parental warmth," "clearly defined limits" and "respectful treatment."

There is considerable literature in which it is argued that these conditions are absent or inconsistently present in the alcoholic home. The alcoholic parent's behavior is affected by the chemicals within, and the non-alcoholic parent's behavior is affected by reaction to the alcoholic. Little emotional energy to consistently fulfill the many needs of children who became victims to the family illness.[5]

People read and are touched by these books because they speak to the problems and anxieties that so many of us have and are struggling with - few people are exempt.

The key to the healing of this rampant disease of compulsive and obsessive behavior in our society is to be found in the tremendous insights gained into dysfunctional behavior at the many chemical dependency treatment centers across the nation. The chemically dependent family provides the model for the addictive society; the dysfunction, the games, the roles and the progressive deterioration are the same. The impressive fact that there are hundreds of thousands of families recovering from this disease should also give us hope for the future.

Religious Addiction: There is an aspect of compulsive behavior that is rarely discussed or spoken about and yet I believe we are all conscious of the pain, devastation and scandal that can ensue when it is not understood or treated seriously. I am talking about religious addiction!

Why is it not talked about? Many people would never consider using the word "addiction" in connection with God, religion, or a church because they would argue that it is difficult to know when pious devotion becomes addiction, or when dedicated discipleship deteriorates into obsessive behavior. Still others would consider it impossible to adequately define a religious addiction or know when a person had it.

People made similar comments years ago concerning alcoholism. What is the difference between a heavy drinker and an alcoholic? How do you define addiction? Isn't self-discipline all that is required for recovery from drug problems? Isn't alcohol abuse the symptom of some underlying emotional disorder that, if discussed and treated, would enable the patient to return to social drinking? Therefore, the questions, arguments and debate that will ensue concerning what I choose to call "religious addiction" should take place within the context of the tremendous success that has been achieved in the field of chemical dependency by the acceptance of the "disease model." Vernon Johnson states in *I'll Quit Tomorrow:*

This disease involves the whole person: physically, mentally, psychologically, and spiritually. The most significant characteristics of the disease are that it is primary, progressive, chronic, and fatal. But it can be arrested. The progress of alcoholism can be stopped, and the patient can be recovered. Not cured, but recovered. This is a hard-headed, pragmatic statement of fact which has visible proof in the recovery of thousands of alcoholics who are well today. They are alive, and they bring alive hope for countless others. Their return gives the lie to the notion that this illness is too complex and too individual by nature even to tackle.[6]

Some people have argued that, whereas chemical dependency is obviously destructive and dangerous, cannot the same be said about a dependency on God or religion? The purpose of this book is to answer precisely that question. I am certainly not wanting to suggest that all religious people are religious addicts, but it is the absence of balance that begins to trigger the dysfunction.

The research that has been done over the past decade concerning compulsive behavior and obsessive relationships (co-dependency), including the effects that follow growing up as a child in a dysfunctional home, strongly supports and affirms my argument that our relationship with God can be co-dependent and our relationship with religion, worship and the church can be as dysfunctional as any chemically dependent family. Yes, people get hooked on God and religion!

In the book, *Co-Dependency: An Emerging Issue,* Robert Subby suggests that co-dependency is:

...an emotional, psychological, and behavioral condition that develops as a result of an individual's prolonged exposure to and practice of a set of oppressive rules - rules that prevent the open expression of feelings as well as the direct discussion of personal and interpersonal problems.[7]

That statement directly points the way to a consideration of religious addiction. Nobody needs doubt that some of these oppressive rules would spring from a rigid religious environment.

If we look at the constant preaching, lecturing, condemning, judging, shame messages, guilt trips, and uninterpreted Biblical texts that pour out of pulpits across the nation, who could doubt that some people would feel sinful, fearful, and ashamed; buried under an avalanche of "oppressive rules." In this sick religious atmosphere we see the nurturing of a dysfunctional relationship with a wrathful and judgmental God. A healthy self-worth would be demolished into nothingness. Shame has entered through the door of religion.

Isn't this type of religion destructive and dangerous? We see that a person can experience the same powerlessness and unmanageability in a dysfunctional relationship with God and religion as from any chemical man has pushed up his nose, stuck in his arm, or guzzled down his throat.

The examples of religious dysfunction are numerous:

The pain and anguish that must have affected the Swaggart family and congregations of the Assemblies of God when they heard and read the Jimmy Swaggart confessions.

The anger of the PTL members concerning the use

and abuse of funds contributed for the furtherance of the Gospel message.

Consider the mass suicide of the congregation that followed the Rev. Jim Jones to Guyana.

Take a penetrating look at the obsessing crowds that surround the Ayatullah Khomeini.

See the mixture of fear, anxieties and "control" in the religious parents who refuse medical treatment for their ailing children.

Listen to the countless stories of addicts and alcoholics who were told by clergymen that they were not sick; all they needed was faith. They should repent for their evil ways and trust in the Lord. Then, after a hastily-arranged healing service, they were pronounced cured, only to be found weeks later shaking in a detox bed, angry, guilty, and alone.

Hear from the women who had married alcoholics, and when they sought help from their priest or pastor, they were not directed to a self-help support meeting or a therapist but to the Bible.

Why don't people talk about religious addiction? There are a number of reasons:

(i) Because many people were brought up not to talk about religion. Religion was a subject that could cause rifts in families or friendships and so it was left alone. The maxim many of us were raised with was,

BREAKING THE CHAINS

"Never talk about religion or politics."
(ii) Some people were taught that if they doubted or criticized religion, they were doubting or criticizing God.
(iii) Many people are ignorant about the Bible. They remember some specific stories from the Old Testament and New Testament but can rarely quote accurately or in context, often getting prophets and apostles confused. This ignorance allows them to become the victims of those who claim "to know."
(iv) The Constitution of the United States safeguards religious liberty, and this means that people can believe whatever they wish. Unfortunately, those who can afford to buy air time on television often create programs that are outrageous in content, allowing no reference or discussion of theological issues. Indeed, often they ridicule academic studies or Christian philosophical insights. They have learned it is the quick fix that produces the money!

Tragically, at different periods in the life of the church (and I would suspect this is true if we were to examine the history of other religions), control over the masses has been sustained by fear—the fear of upsetting God or being condemned to Hell. This same fear and reticence pervades areas of Western society today. And, although in the realm of politics it has lost its force with the birth of "one man, one vote" and the establishment of democracy, still, with religion, we are presented with an authoritarian theocracy where the "few," the "chosen," and the "called" control the many. This divinely appointed power group claims not only to speak "for" God but insists on leading the people "to" God. Such an attitude restricts debate and discussion. Catholics avoid criticizing the Pope or Church for fear of appearing critical of God and tradition. Likewise, with many of the Protestant denominations, we see how the power of the preachers or the elders is guarded with a ferociousness that the tribes of Israel once displayed to protect the Ark of the Covenant.

But this religious power structure is beginning to reveal some cracks. The fundamentalist Christians have found it difficult to defend or justify many of their Biblical positions in the face of the research achievements from modern science. Also since Vatican II, the Roman Catholic Church has been receiving criticism from a number of independent groups which, when added together, become a sizable force for change. And recently, another crack has appeared from an unlikely source - the TV evangelist.

Television is the most powerful marketing agent in the world. The manufactured product, at the switch of a button, comes into the homes of millions. Television encourages us to buy. It presents an attractive and irresistible package. It appeals to that part of us that doesn't want to miss a bargain - a chance in a lifetime! The TV evangelist is also involved in this media salesmanship. He presents God, Jesus and the church as a commodity that everybody needs and should have. The services, music and testimonies appeal to every emotion. For millions, the message is irresistible -people believe they can not live without it. Naturally, the financial contributions that are collected from the viewers are astronomical and the power of the TV evangelist has spread across the nation. Everyday, at any hour, you can find a preacher telling you how to "find" God; conducting a service where those who are sick are seen to be healed by faith, where the promise of eternity and prosperity are within your grasp - *and only by giving, (financially) will you receive!*

It is television that keeps the preachers in control. In their pulpits, they are six feet above contradiction, with an influence that reaches into the homes of millions. Their ministries have become even more visible, national and lucrative. The lowly traveling preacher of yesterday who went from town to town and pitched his tent in the market place has become a public figure recognized by millions. The "holy" man is no longer isolated in the desert or majestic cathedral - he has become the property of the media that created and sustained him. In a way, it is similar to the Frankenstein story; the preacher has created a powerful specimen (TV ministry) that has made him famous. But that same creation can also be the means of his destruction. It was, therefore, only a matter of time before the "sinful" preacher (nobody is perfect) was caught with the unacceptable sin; and it happened. The scandals that have enveloped Jim and Tammy Bakker, followed closely by the sex scandal of Jimmy Swaggart - which have necessarily reverberated into all the TV ministries and churches across the nation - have served to highlight the complex nature of compulsive excesses. The preacher was caught with his hand in the cookie jar, so to speak.

Time magazine reported:

...the couple (Jim and Tammy Bakker) received nearly $1.6 million in pay last year from their PTL (for Praise the Lord or People That Love) television ministry. In the first three months of this year... the Pentecostal preacher and his wife received $640,000. In all, the Bakkers were paid $4.8 million in salary, bonuses and other compensation between 1984 and last month.[8]

Newsweek magazine reported the holdings of the PTL to:

...include a rare 1939 Rolls-Royce and a house in Tega Cay, S.C. Value: $1.5 million. (The Bakkers own four condos, homes in California and in Tennessee, and two Mercedes-Benzes.)[9]

Newsweek magazine also reported in its May 4, 1987, issue:

The preacher (Jimmy Swaggart) spent less than 10 percent (of $20 million raised for a children's fund) on the program.... "The rest was spent in Baton Rouge," where, WBRZ-TV reports, the Swaggart compound includes Jimmy's $1 million home, his son's $776,000 spread and his grandchild's air-conditioned tree house.[10]

For the first time in a long while, society, the people, were given permission to ask questions, to think and be angry. Not only was the church on trial, not only were preachers to be held accountable, but institutional religion itself, its claims, its message, its power and how it maintained its power, were to be scrutinized.

Many registered their disapproval with TV ministries and stopped their financial support. However, other people remained and the money continued to pour in. The P.T.L. Club raised millions in a matter of weeks.

People continued to defend and support the bizarre claims of some of the preachers. *Time* magazine reported the extravagant claims of Rev. Oral Roberts:

The controversy produced by those episodes, however, has been overshadowed by Roberts' latest extraordinary claim: God has used him to raise the dead. Before an audience of 6,000 at Oral Roberts University, the evangelist said, "I've had to stop a sermon, go back and raise a dead person," adding good-naturedly, "It did improve my altar call that night." Roberts provided no details. Later, his son Richard, 38, expanded the revivication claim, asserting that in 50 or 60 cases Oral and other ministers had raised the dead.[11]

Tammy Bakker confessed not only to being a drug addict but also to being a compulsive shopper. It was reported in *Newsweek* magazine:

. . . Tammy's most effective remedy for stress, both then and now, was the same as Imelda Marcos's: shopping up a storm. "It's a kind of a hobby to help my nerves," she explained on Nightline last week. After an exhausting show, she once said, "My shoppin' demons are hoppin'," and she dashes off to the mall. Getting a good deal is part of the fun; her CB handle was "The Bargain-hunter." . . . "There's times I just have to quit thinking," she explains in "Christian Wives," "and the only way I can quit thinking is by shopping.[12]

And still the money poured in.

Then Swaggart's sex scandal broke. *Time* reported in its March 7, 1988, issue:

It was, without question, the most dramatic sermon ever aired on television. There stood Jimmy Swaggart, 52, the king of evangelistic video, ready to confront the ugly rumors that were encircling his busy, buzzing gospel conglomerate. As he approached the pulpit, the octagonal Family Worship Center in Baton Rouge, La., was packed for the occasion with 8,000 worshipers, 1,000 of them standees, while followers nationwide watched the weekly telecast. This day there was to be none of Swaggart's trademark piano riffing or gospel singing, none of his jig stepping, strutting or shouting. Clad in a severe suit, the TV evangelist waited quietly, then began to speak.

"I do not call it a mistake, a mendacity. I call it a sin. . . I have no one but myself to blame," he intoned. . . .

Then, finally, he spoke directly to "my Savior, my Redeemer...I have sinned against you, my Lord, and I would ask that your precious blood would wash and cleanse every stain until it is in the seas of God's forgiveness, never to be remembered against me anymore."

...At no point did Swaggart utter a word about what his sin was. But the entire world was already learning about sexual indiscretions committed over an extended period by this specialist in denouncing sins of the flesh. Swaggart stood accused of strange, secret involvements with prostitutes in sleazy motels. His own church body acted after being confronted with incriminating photographs.

This revelation and confession concerning the secret life of Jimmy Swaggart was even more duplicitous when we recall his statement some six months earlier concerning the impossibility, for him, of any sexual indiscretion. Swaggart told *Time* magazine, "Frances (his wife) is with me all the time. She goes to every crusade we go to, and if she doesn't go, I have several people who go with me. I'm never alone. I'm never by myself." The hypocrisy is underlined when we recall Jimmy Swaggart's sentiments concerning the necessary moral character of a preacher of the gospel, recorded in his magazine *The Evangelist,* written during the time he was involved in seeing and paying the prostitute, Debra Murphree, to perform sexual acts while he watched. Swaggart wrote in the article:

To allow a preacher of the Gospel, when he is caught beyond a shadow of a doubt committing an immoral act...to remain in his position as pastor (or whatever), would be the most gross stupidity. Under the rules of the Assemblies of God, such a sinner must be suspended from preaching for one year and put on probation for a second year, or else there is a danger that the whole church will be destroyed.

The symptoms of religious addiction and abuse

became evident. Naturally, as we have seen with other compulsions, the religious addict denied there were any serious problems or financial irregularities. They condemned the media for exaggerating the situation, continued to solicit donations, isolated themselves into a "holy huddle" and used religious texts and the name of Jesus to fend off any criticisms.

Mavis Peterson, a retiree in Springfield, Mo., who has watched the Jimmy Swaggart program for a decade, was quoted in the March issue of *Time:* "Brother Swaggart is an imperfect human being, but the Bible says those who love the Lord and seek the truth shall have their sins forgiven if they repent."

Mickey Gilley, Swaggart's cousin, said after hearing the confession, "I admire him for confessing the way he did, in front of his church. It takes a lot to stand in front of a congregation and pull something out of your soul like that." (*People* magazine, March, 7, 1988)

Swaggart's aunt, Edna Mequet, of Mandeville, La., said in the same article:

> To tell you the truth, it made me sick. My blood pressure shot way up. But somehow God can take things that are wrong, like this problem, and turn them around to His glory.
>
> If it's true, maybe that's why he preached so hard against it for so long, because he knew what a grip it could get on you. Jimmy's daddy said that this might help Jimmy learn not to be so critical of others. I think maybe this will make Jimmy a better man, a more humble minister. Maybe now he won't be so hard on people.
>
> It just goes to show that none of us is so high that we can't fall, and maybe that's what God is trying to show us with this.

The "dysfunctional family" was on the defense.

But many found it too painful and began to recognize and talk about the "slavery" that they had been caught up in. They realized their religious obsession and sought help for their compulsive behavior. And although the scandal surrounding the TV evangelists was like a small mustard seed in the field of religious addiction, it was soon to grow and affect religion in America. People began to talk about being addicted around a church, a concept of God, a TV evangelist or a rigid interpretation of the Bible. Some people went on television and discussed how, after the devastation caused by the evangelist scandal, they were made to see how their Christian behavior and attitude was similar to how they had behaved years before around alcohol and drugs. They exemplified the theory of cross-addiction. Many addictionologists see in the Jimmy Swaggart scandal the symptom of a sexual addiction — an obsession concerning pornography that had haunted the evangelist for years.

The religious addicts had simply changed addictions or added religion to their list of compulsions. They were still looking for "a fix." They had become "hooked" on religion.

Many recovering co-dependents and adult children of alcoholics who, for years, had grappled with their fear and anxiety exacerbated by an overdemanding and controlling alcoholic parent or spouse, saw a similar relationship developing in their fear and anxiety towards God. The same denial, isolation, low self-esteem and anger - all hidden behind a televised "Gospel grin."

The controversy created by Oral Roberts asking for $8.5 million or he would be "taken home," the Jim and Tammy Bakker financial and sex scandals, followed by Jimmy Swaggart's involvement with a prostitute, had unconsciously created a national intervention that has affected religion in America. Religious addiction and religious abuse, until now recognized by only a few, was finally being seriously examined.

Questions were being asked, religious statements were examined. Finances were being audited and local newspapers were printing angry letters from the poor, the elderly, and the lonely. The TV evangelists were asked to be accountable.

As an addictionologist and a student of theology, I realized that just as it made sense to talk about "a dysfunctional family" or "a dysfunctional society," now we needed also to talk about a dysfunctional belief system, religion and church.

Scripture can be abused,
   Religion can be abused,
      God can be abused.

This is said not in the spirit of casting stones. If any one us had had the public scrutiny that followed Oral Roberts, Jim and Tammy Bakker, and Jimmy Swaggart, few of us would come out of it smelling like roses. The point is that to talk about the extravagances and autocratic control exercised by many evangelists and not to examine or appreciate the dynamics of religious addiction and abuse is to have missed a "learning moment." The sickness that generates religious abuse can respond to treatment just as other addictions have benefited from treatment.

As a recovering alcoholic, I am aware of the many aspects of denial that keep people sick and dysfunctional, and they are particularly true in the area of religion. Those who claim to have the "only way" are scary because they avoid the reality of change. A basic history of religion and Christianity should teach us that no one group of people in this universe has all the answers. A Hindu teacher, the late Baba Muktananda said:

Every religion is okay in its own right. There may be many religions - not hundreds, but thousands of religions. Yet, how many Gods are there to bestow their grace upon all these religious people? God is One - He can't become two. Does God belong to the Hindus? Is He a Christian? Is He Jewish? Is He a Sufi? Does He belong to Buddhism? Is He black? Is He red? Is He white? To whom does He belong? This is the important question, and it is worth contemplating.

Now it is very likely that because He is God He belongs to everybody. For Hindus, He is Ram. For the Christians He is called God. For Sufis, He is Allah, and for the Zoroastrians, He is Zarathustra. Everyone calls Him by a different name.

After pursuing all these religions, we should learn how to cultivate the awareness of Universal Brotherhood. Don't pursue these religions so that we can murder one another with distinctions. All countries belong to Him, and all languages belong to Him. He belongs to everybody. All the people who follow different religions should attain this understanding.[13]

Traditionally, the religious quest for Truth has involved the dynamic concepts of change and dialogue. However, for religious addicts, such a statement is too liberal, wishy-washy, and comprehensive. They insist upon a more narrow, rigid and exclusive understanding of faith that necessarily creates division. Interestingly enough, Jesus Christ, in His teachings, seemed to be consciously aware of these dangers. Constantly He reminded His disciples to guard against "hypocrisy" and religious arrogance. He was preoccupied with exposing those people who pretended to be what they were not, those who escaped from reality into fantasy and who denied what was truly happening in their lives. Jesus condemned murder, blasphemy, adultery, stealing - but it should be remembered that a great amount of his ministry was concerned with condemning hypocrisy, especially religious hypocrisy.

So the Lord said to him, "Now then, you Pharisees, clean the outside of your cup and plate, but inside you are full of violence and evil. Fools! Did not God, who made the outside, also make the inside? But give what is in your cups and plates to the poor, and everything will be ritually clean for you.

"How terrible for you Pharisees! You give to God one tenth of the seasoning herbs, such as mint and rue and all the other herbs, but you neglect justice and love for God. These you should practice, without neglecting the others.

"How terrible for you Pharisees! You love the reserved seats in the synagogues and to be greeted with respect in the marketplaces. How terrible for you! You are like unmarked graves which people walk without knowing it."

One of the teachers of the Law said to him, "Teacher, when you say this, you insult us, too!" Jesus answered, "How terrible also for you as teachers of the Law! You put onto people's backs loads which are hard to carry, but you yourselves will not stretch out a finger to help them carry those loads. How terrible for you! You make fine tombs for the prophets - the very prophets your ancestors murdered. You yourselves admit, then, that you approve of what your ancestors did; they murdered the prophets, and you build their tombs. For this reason the Wisdom of God said, 'I will send them prophets and messengers; they will kill some of them and persecute others.'" (Luke 11:38-49)

"How terrible for you teachers of the Law! You have kept the key that opens the door to the house of knowledge; you yourselves will not go in, and you stop those who are trying to go in!" (Luke 11:52)

Such statements need to be explained and interpreted within the context of their times. But I cannot help feeling that these admonitions are applicable for many religious people today.

I am not suggesting that all religious people who go to church, synagogue or mosque are religious addicts or have been religiously abused, but I do believe a significant percentage of them have a dysfunctional belief system. How do I know? I have met them, spoken with them, read and discussed their stories in therapy groups, not to mention encountering them over the years at church socials, railway stations, and at airports.

In the last few years, I have been aware of the similarities between those who are addicted to drugs, alcohol, sex, people (co-dependency), and the growing number who are addicted to God, to religion, to a belief system, or to a preacher. In the chemical dependency treatment centers, I have met a number of alcoholics and addicts who reveal a rigid compulsion concerning religion that signals an aspect of compulsive behavior. They make statements like...

God has taken over my life and I know I will never drink again.

Only through the Lord Jesus Christ can a man be guaranteed sobriety and serenity.

If you do not accept the Holy Spirit, you are condemned to Hell.

The spiritual life of the Twelve Steps must be linked to Jesus Christ.

I did not need treatment for my addiction in a hospital. I went to God the Healer and confessed my sins.

Jews and Catholics are going to hell because they do not accept the Bible.

These statements did not come from any one religion or Christian denomination. And although I was offended by their arrogance and divisiveness, I needed to appreciate the atmosphere and background in which they were nurtured. It is not unusual for influential preachers and leaders of religious movements to make arrogant statements that the naive and insecure would consider the Word of God. Louis Farrakhan has stated:

I have a problem with the Jewish people . . . they are not the chosen people of God. (*Los Angeles Times,* March 3, 1986)

He has also called Adolf Hitler "wickedly great" and Judaism a "dirty" and "gutter" religion. (*USA Today,* August 5, 1987).

One of the most controversial of the television pastors, Jimmy Swaggart, has condemned the Supreme Court and Congress ("institutions damned by God") and Roman Catholicism ("a false cult"). He once advised an audience, "Don't ever bargain with Jesus. He's a Jew."[14]

And now the statement that he is surely living to regret, concerning his condemnation of Jim Bakker: "I'm ashamed, I'm embarrassed. The Gospel of Jesus Christ has never sunk to such a level as it is today." (*Newsweek,* Feb. 29, 1988).

Jimmy Swaggart can only hope that his fellow Christians take a more charitable view of his own indiscretions.

A movement within the Roman Catholic church that has been referred to as "John Paul's shock troops" is called Opus Dei (God's Work). *Newsweek* magazine reported:

Although Opus Dei emphasizes the supernatural significance of ordinary life, the movement has adopted some exotic and often controversial practices. Opus Dei encourages its unmarried members to flagellate themselves periodically with meterlong leather whips and to wear the "cilicio," a chain-mail band, about the thigh or waist. In "The Way," the movement's handbook of 999 aphorisms that the faithful find inspired but critics consider insipid, Escriva (founder of the movement who died in 1975) urges members to behave as spiritual "children." When the movement's leaders decide on a course of action, its members must follow. "In apostolic work," Escriva teaches, "there is no such thing as a trifling disobedience." "Anyone who commits himself totally to Opus Dei and then decides to leave," says Michael Barrett, a 30-year-old numerary from New York City, "is regarded as a defector, just like a priest who marries or a man who abandons his wife."[15]

During the same article, it was stated:

As a result, the movement has been likened by critics to a fifth column within the church - a suspicion shared by many bishops. "What I don't like is their secrecy," says one U.S. prelate. Indeed, last year the British Catholic Primate, Cardinal Basil Hume published guidelines for his diocese that requires Opus Dei to permit members to select their own spiritual directors and, if they choose, to leave the movement freely.[16]

A large number of people who become religious addicts, or have been religiously abused, grew up against a background of chemical dependency either directly, in that they are alcoholic, or were raised in an alcoholic or addicted family environment. Developing the insights gained from the research carried out within the "Adult Children of Alcoholics Movement," we see that many religious addicts grew up in dysfunctional homes where they were neglected, abandoned, or abused (physically, mentally, emotionally, and sexually). I also believe that many of these children were religiously abused. Growing up in the chaos and pain of such a home would naturally plant the seed of escape - and more than a few escaped into religion. They escaped to a God who would take them out of this sinful world; to a God who was gentle, kind and non-physical; to a spiritual power who condemned the wicked and banished them to Hell.

Why are we surprised? At some level, all addicts or co-dependents are escaping or wanting to escape from reality. They escape into a world of fantasy. They refuse to accept the pain in their lives, minimizing or denying the guilt and shame of physical, sexual and religious abuse. Unhappy about what they understand the world to be about, they are pessimistic about life and happiness, resentful and angry that they did not have a home or family like so many of their friends. They desperately wanted a father or mother who would love them without conditions. I am suggesting that many of these children escaped through an addictive religion into the "next world."

God became their drug of choice.

God had chosen them from all the others.

They craved a belief in Heaven that would take them away from a living Hell.

They developed an exaggerated attitude towards personal purity to ensure a sanctified redemption.

They became "hooked" on an all-consuming discipleship that required either total conversion or eternal damnation.

Again I ask, why be surprised? We know that growing up in a dysfunctional system creates dysfunction. Children from dysfunctional homes create relationships where they continue to be abused. Often they marry alcoholics and/or drug abusers or create relationships where they are neglected. Many children from dysfunctional homes become compulsive overeaters, workaholics, gamblers, sex addicts, and develop the disease of co-dependency, destroying any personal self-esteem or self-worth. And many abuse themselves in a religion that keeps them separate, angry, isolated, guilty and ashamed. They claim or seek unattainable purity, become dependent upon certain texts of the Bible and condemn unconverted family, friends and co-workers to Hell.

I am suggesting that many people who have developed a religious addiction have previously had problems with drugs or alcohol, or were nurtured in a dysfunctional home. The dysfunction might not have specifically involved drugs, but may have taken the form of being "smothered" from childhood in a home where the religious belief system was narrow, rigid and exclusive. For many, everything in the world seemed to be either "sinful" or "forbidden" - with the possible exception of food. The one thing you were allowed to do was eat, and many ate with a passion!

Although eating disorders are being discussed in the media, and are being treated at many chemical dependency treatment centers, the general public has little understanding of the disease. Many people still see the fat person as a happy person or a figure of fun. Too many addicts shy away from identifying their own eating disorders, particularly religious addicts.

Why would a religious addict turn to food? I think the

main reason is that other drugs or chemicals are usually taboo. Growing up in a strict religious atmosphere would prohibit the use of tobacco, alcohol, cocaine, heroin, and marijuana.

Many children who suffered religious abuse were not allowed to dance, listen to music, or develop significant relationships with the opposite sex until they were engaged or married. However, the one thing they were allowed to do, and were usually encouraged to do, was eat. A significant number of people who have a religious addiction, or grew up in a family where religious addiction was evident, develop an eating disorder. Extreme religious groups, who consider the use of alcohol, tobacco and drugs an abuse of the body, seem to ignore the chronic abuse of compulsive overeating. God's kingdom - and a donut, too!

I make this observation because many readers, who had thought they had no history of drug or chemical abuse in their family, might reconsider when they examine their eating habits. Certainly, they might be willing to look at the connection between their eating and the repression of feelings produced by their religion.

In my book *Spirituality and Recovery,* I described a woman I helped treat in an eating disorder unit. Elizabeth was very close to developing a religious addiction that would have been as painful and as devastating for her life as her eating disorder. It might be helpful to look at Elizabeth's story:

During her childhood, Elizabeth learned how to eat. Eating brought satisfaction. Comfort. Relief. More eating, more comfort. Enormous eating, enormous satisfaction. She sneaked food. She hid food. Minimized amounts. Food became her protection from people. Protection from criticism. Eventually, food took her on a "trip" away from her pain, away from reality.

Elizabeth spoke about her understanding of religion. It told her she was a sinner...needing repentance...needing salvation. She was told that she was no good without Jesus...without the Holy Spirit...without the Bible. The conditions of Heaven were purity and obedience. Her fears were perceived as guilt. Being human became a sin. However, nothing was said about food. Sex was a sin...thinking sex was terrible...nothing was said about food. It was okay to eat. Eating felt good and the more the better.

Elizabeth was such a good eater. Elizabeth's eating made her grandmother proud. Grandmother told her she was chubby and happy...fat people are happy. She wanted to stay happy, so she ate.

When Elizabeth went to visit friends, she learned how to please the people. She ate all...They all smiled. She painfully remembered that once she said "no more." Everybody looked disappointed. Had she insulted the host? Guilt. Feelings of rejection. She would never say "no more" again. Never disappoint grandmother. Never disappoint her friends again. She learned how to eat everything and vomit afterwards. Always in anger, guilt, loneliness or fear she would return to food. Even when her anger, guilt and loneliness were caused by food, she would return to food. Everything would revolve around food.

In the hospital, Elizabeth began to talk about this story. She began to see her disease come alive in her written words. She wrote down her feelings and owned them. She discovered forgotten feelings. Feelings she had swallowed with food. Buried with the food. Hid in the food. Elizabeth faced reality, then she cried.

She came to see, understand, and accept the disease process. Her drug is food. Like the drinking alcoholic, she would hide it. Deny it. Lie about it. Lose her job over it. Get divorced over it. Suffer using it. Food was her mind-altering drug. Food instantly works. Food brings satisfaction. Food is instant escape. This is Addiction.

Elizabeth was not a bad, crazy, ugly, sinful, irresponsible girl and woman. She was sick. She needed help. She felt she was utterly alone. In the hospital, she met fellow sufferers. People who were being treated for the same disease. The symptoms were the same.

The pain the same. The growing numbers of people were demanding recognition for their disease.

In a treatment center, we helped Elizabeth treat her disease.
However, Elizabeth must do the work, make recovery happen. We
could be like treating a bullet wound with a Band-Aid. . . Elizabeth
needed more. When a patient needs surgery, you do not give a pill.
Elizabeth needed surgery.

In order to create a realistic food program, we needed from
Elizabeth honesty, willingness, cooperation.

We needed to hear her stuffed feelings:
> fear,
>> resentment,
>>> loneliness,
>>>> and anger.

We needed Elizabeth to see that in these feelings was the
disease. The food was the symptom. All the pain, all the feelings of
being "less than," all the people-pleasing had to be seen and
owned. All the denial, the manipulation, the self pity had to be seen
and owned. This is treatment.[17]

Elizabeth's religion before entering treatment was not
helpful. Rather, it was repressive and kept her feeling
dirty, guilty and ashamed. Today when I talk with
people seeking help for a religious addiction, whether
for themselves or a loved one, I hear the same words:
"feeling lonely, guilty and ashamed." The painful
emotions that propelled them to seek a religious "fix"
from God, religion or a priest continue to keep their lives
dysfunctional. It is my hope that those who are being
treated for an eating disorder or any other compulsive
behavior will consider and examine their religious
attitudes. A religious compulsion rarely exists in
isolation from other compulsions.

For those of us who have admitted and accepted a
recognized addiction, we need to be particularly aware
of the danger of transferring one compulsive behavior

pattern onto another. A significant number of cocaine addicts, who rarely abused alcohol when they snorted cocaine, discovered that when they abstained from cocaine they developed a dependency upon alcohol. Thousands of ex-smokers talk about developing an obsession around food (usually candies or ice cream) after they had put down cigarettes. Indeed, I have heard people use their fear of overeating and gaining weight as an excuse for continued smoking!

As I have suggested earlier in this book, it is probable that Jimmy Swaggart had a compulsion concerning pornography that caused him immense emotional pain, which he sought to remove with a compulsive, aggressive and rigid religion. Clearly, treatment and continued therapy is necessary alongside repentance. Today, addictionologists in many chemical dependency treatment centers are discussing not only their patients' obsession around drugs and alcohol, but other obsessions as well. Brenda Schaeffer, in *Is It Love or Is It Addiction?*, states:

> In my opinion, there are other kinds of addictions that hamper our lives and these are rarely recognized or addressed. Some become bigger problems than others. The list of things to which people become addicted includes food, exercise, spending money, religious cults, psychotherapy, nicotine, sugar, caffeine, sex, gambling, work, television, pain, illness, parenting and love objects. Perhaps you recognize an obsession of your own among them.[18]

And I would suggest that mainline religious denominations, churches and God be included: anything can be abused.

Relapse: We also need to consider religious addiction in the context of relapse and prevention. Many addicts who have relapsed, or found themselves near relapse after some period of recovery, talked about identifiable obsessions around other things. They avoided talking about loneliness, anxiety and fear; stuffing their feelings behind food, work and sex; experiencing outbursts of anger and rage that could easily lead to relapse. The bottom line was the pain in their lives.

An unhealthy approach to God, a compulsive behavior pattern around a church or belief system, an obsession with religious tracts or an evangelist can also indicate a "state of relapse." An abuse of God is an abuse of self and vice versa. A program of recovery from any addiction requires that we have a responsible and realistic use and interpretation of the Bible; a responsible and realistic understanding of God. To hide behind God, religion or prophetic pronouncements is manipulation and indicates a state of relapse.

There are times in the course of this book when I shall make references to religions other than Christianity. I do this because religious addiction is not limited to any one religion or culture. However, because most of the religious addicts we meet belong to the numerous denominations within Christianity, it is inevitable that an abuse of Jesus, the Church and Holy Scripture will dominate these pages.

The purpose of this book is not to dispense with God, but to stop an abuse of God. It is not to destroy religion, but to discover the challenge and adventure it provides in the here and now. It is not to ridicule discipleship, but rather to encourage development of a creative relationship with God that allows for personal responsibility and change, enabling one to discover the Power that exists within all of us.

FOOTNOTES

1. Schaef, Ann Wilson, *When Society Becomes an Addict.* (San Francisco, Harper & Row, 1985) p.4.
2. Ibid, p.5.
3. Norwood, Robin, *Women Who Love Too Much - When you keep wishing and hoping he'll change.* (New York, Simon & Schuster, 1985) p. XIV.
4. Schaeffer, Brenda, *Is It Love or Is It Addiction?* (Hazelden, 1987) p. 5.
5. Woititz, Janet Geringer, *Adult Children of Alcoholics,* (Pompano Beach, Fla., Health Communications, 1983) p. 2.
6. Johnson, Vernon E., *I'll Quit Tomorrow.* (San Francisco, Harper & Row, 1980) p. 1.
7. Subby, Robert, *Co-dependency - An Emerging Issue.* (Pompano Beach, Fla., Health Communications, 1984) p. 28.
8. Brand, David, "An 'Outrageous' Ministry." *Time,* Vol. 130. (May 4, 1987) p. 82.
9. "Heaven Can Wait." *Newsweek,* (June 8, 1987) p. 59.
10. "What Profits a Preacher." *Newsweek,* (May 4, 1987) p. 68.
11. Ostling, Richard N. "Raising Eyebrows and the Dead." *Time,* Vol. 130, (July 13, 1987) p. 55.
12. Seligman, Jean, "The Inimitable Tammy Faye," *Newsweek,* (June 8, 1987) p. 69.
13. Booth, Fr. Leo, *Spirituality and Recovery - Walking on Water,* (Pompano Beach, Fla., Health Communications, 1985) p.36-37.
14. Ostling, Richard N. "TV's holy row: a sex and money scandal tarnishes electronic evangelism (Jim Bakker affair)." *Time.* Vol. 129. (April 6, 1987) p. 60-65.
15. Woodward, Kenneth L. and Carolyn Friday, "John Paul's Shock Troops." *Newsweek,* Vol. 100, (September 20, 1982) p. 88.
16. Ibid.
17. Booth, Fr. Leo, *Spirituality and Recovery - Walking on Water,* (Pompano Beach, Fla., Health Communications, 1985) p. 16-18.
18. Schaeffer, Brenda, *Is It Love or Is It Addiction?* (Minneapolis, Hazelden, 1987) Preface.

Chapter 2

DYSFUNCTIONAL BEHAVIOR

Let us look at the problem of religious addiction in the context of what we have learned from other compulsive and obsessive behavior patterns.

Addiction is an escape: Addiction is an absence of balance. That thin line is crossed between enjoyment and craving. Whatever the reasons, excuses or circumstances that might be given, people who use drugs or become compulsive around a person, persons or thing are looking for a "fix" - something from the outside to make them feel good inside; something that they believe will help them face their problems or relieve their anxieties; something to add strength and vitality to the meaning of their lives. It is not too dramatic to say that addiction is an inherited or learned dysfunctional behavior pattern that is based upon fantasy. Millions of people, on a daily basis, escape with a drug or through co-dependency into a world of illusion. They lose their sense of balance. And they begin to experience pain and distress as the craving and obsession progress. Yet the approaching catastrophe is hidden behind a facade of:

"Everything is fine."

"I'm in control."

"I've never felt better."

This "addictive behavioral mechanism" is called an illness, a disease. The medical credibility for understanding compulsive behavior as a disease is found in the 1956 American Medical Association directive concerning alcoholism that was released by the Board of Trustees:

Among the numerous personality disorders encountered in the general population, it has long been recognized that a vast number of such disorders are characterized by the outstanding sign of excessive use of alcohol. All excessive users of alcohol are not diagnosed as alcoholics, but all alcoholics are excessive users. When, in addition to this excessive use, there are certain signs and symptoms of behavioral, personality and physical disorders...the syndrome of alcoholism is achieved. The intoxication and some of the other possible complications manifested in this syndrome often make treatment difficult. However, alcoholism must be regarded as within the purview of medical practice. The Council on Mental Health, its Committee on Alcoholism, and the profession in general recognizes this syndrome as illness [disease] which justifiably should have the attention of physicians.[1]

This definition of alcoholism is the basis for understanding and treating other compulsive behaviors as diseases that have observable symptoms. Only when we begin to examine and treat the symptoms of the disease will people begin to heal. Many addictionologists have argued that a treatment modality that incorporates a Twelve-Step philosophy enjoys a greater success. Dr. Le Clair Bissell and Paul W. Haberman published some scientific data concerning the alcoholic professional and A.A. in their book *Alcoholism in the Professions*. They write:

At first interview, there was a wide variation in the number of A.A. meetings that individuals attended. This was influenced by the size of the community, the availability of groups, whether a spouse belongs to A.A. or Alanon, and whether the respondent was involved in treating other alcoholics. Nonetheless, 97 percent of the 407 subjects said they had attended A.A. meetings one or more times in the previous year. Three-fifths attended meetings at least once a week, and 5 percent of these went to meetings daily.

Frequency of attendance was inversely related to the length of abstinence. Those more newly sober tended to go to meetings more frequently than those who had been abstinent for a longer time. Those who went to very few meetings were often apologetic, saying they felt they probably should go more often and were anxious not to be seen as considering themselves good examples.

Its members do not refer to A.A. as "treatment," although outsiders often do. It is a fellowship in which there is little obvious power structure and in which members relate to one another as peers. One is not expected to complete a process, as one does with treatment; hence one is free to remain part of the group indefinitely without any need to finish a particular task or to advance in the hierarchy. No records are kept. There are no dues or fees. There are no patients and no therapists.

These various aspects of A.A. cannot be said either to have attracted or repelled our respondents, most of whom initially approached A.A. while knowing very little about it. Most knew only that it was supposed to help, but had only a vague idea of its methods. They were aware that its focus would be on drinking.

All of our subjects eventually went to A.A. About one-half of them (men, 48%; women, 53%) reported at the initial interview that the first A.A. meeting and the last drink occurred at the same time. One-fifth reported no further drinking after their first year in A.A. (19% each for men and women). For the others there were a series of exploratory visits - sometimes even lengthy attendance punctuated with many relapses - before a satisfactory alliance was made and the drinking ended.[2]

Some people have problems understanding or accepting the concept of addiction as a disease because they have such a narrow definition of what constitutes "a disease." Those dysfunctions that cause a deterioration in the liver or pancreas, malfunctions that affect the brain's neuro-transmitter or a physical breakdown in the body's immune system are accepted without question as diseases. Yet understanding compulsive behavior as a disease is not comprehended by the vast majority of people. Certainly, the concept of religious addiction as a progressive disease creates problems for many people.

A way of understanding the concept of disease in relation to compulsive and obsessive behavior is to come at it from a different direction. The word DIS-EASE is the opposite of being AT-EASE. It speaks of a real pain and discomfort in a person's life that causes physical, mental or emotional problems. In this sense the disease is not a germ but an emotional feeling that grows and affects the whole person. When we talk about compulsive behavior as a disease, we do not mean a virus or germ, but rather, a physical, mental and emotional craving that is released in reaction to alcohol, drugs or a relationship. Why? How? When? We do not have all the answers to these questions. However, we are aware of a variety of symptoms that have been checked and cross-checked, and are evidenced in many people living in different situations, coming from a variety of backgrounds and cultures. The symptoms are the same.

Flu is flu, and if you live in America or Jamaica the symptoms will be the same; so it is with alcoholism, cocaine addiction and religious addiction.

Children of alcoholics living in New York sit and talk with children of alcoholics in Toronto and are able to identify with the variety of feelings and resentments.

A compulsive gambler in Wyoming visits a Gamblers Anonymous meeting in London and feels at one with the types of behavior and anxieties discussed.

The disease concept that is demonstrated in alcoholism and other obsessions around chemicals is also evident concerning religious addiction.

The religious addict is not at-ease with God, himself, relationships or his world. He uses God, a church, preacher, scriptural text, TV evangelist, holy message, belief system, guru, or a mystical vision as a means to escape. He discovers in this dysfunctional use of religion that something outside of himself makes him feel good, accepted or powerful. He gets high on being saved. He is hooked on a particular interpretation of the Bible - and lacks tolerance, charity and acceptance for those who do not share his beliefs. He is spaced in his own fantasy world and avoids reality.

Alcoholism affects the whole person and in this sense it has been referred to as a "spiritual disease." Nothing is spared. Every aspect of the alcoholic's life is affected, leaving him like a walking zombie. Dignity, self-esteem, and conscience are disgorged in the vomit! This pain is not only physical, but also involves mental confusion and emotional despair. In Alcoholics Anonymous, we read:

Most of us have been willing to admit we were real alcoholics. No person likes to think he is bodily mentally different from his fellows. Therefore, it is not surprising that our drinking careers have been characterized by countless vain attempts to prove we could drink like other people. The idea that somehow, someday he will control and enjoy his drinking is the great obsession of every abnormal drinker. The persistence of this illusion is astonishing. Many pursue it into the gates of insanity or death.... Here are some of the methods we have tried: Drinking beer only, limiting the number of drinks, never drinking alone, never drinking in the morning, drinking only at home, never having it in the house, never drinking during business hours, drinking only at parties, switching from scotch to brandy, drinking only natural wines, agreeing to resign if ever drunk on the job, taking a trip, not taking a trip, swearing off forever (with and without solemn oath), taking more physical exercise, reading inspirational books, going to health farms and sanitariums, accepting voluntary commitment to asylums - we could increase the list ad infinitum.[3]

A similar devastation haunts the religious addict. I received a letter from a self-confessed religious addict describing how she became aware of her addiction concerning religion and its effects upon her life. She wrote about a progressive infatuation with scriptural texts, an obsession with the truth of her own religious convictions, religious arguments with family and co-workers, eventual isolation from family, culminating in financial embarrassment caused by excessive tithing to her church. Alongside these events she was aware of feeling lonely, angry, depressed, fearful, and guilty. The more she pursued her obsessive religious lifestyle, the more helpless and isolated she became.

As with the alcoholic, this confessed religious addict described similar effects and attempts to break away or stop her obsessive behavior; not going to church, removing crucifixes and Bibles from her home, avoiding religious TV, hiding from members of her congregation, not returning telephone calls from her pastor, canceling subscriptions for religious magazines - but always experiencing, after a period of time, relapse. She wrote, asking for counseling, treatment and "religious detox" in a safe environment.

Dr. E.M. Jellenik categorized the symptoms of alco-

DISEASE OF ALCOHOLISM
Progression

EARLY STAGES

Social drinking.
Increase in alcohol tolerance.

Desire to continue when others stop.

Relief drinking begins.
Preoccupation with alcohol (thinking about the next drink).

Loss of control phase.

Rationalizing begins.

Increasing frequency of relief drinking.

Sneaking drinks.

Drinking bolstered with excuses.

Drinking to calm nerves.
Drinking before a drinking function.

Uncomfortable in situations where there is no alcohol.
Occasional memory lapses after heavy drinking.

Secret irritation when your drinking is discussed.
Lying about drinking.

Hiding liquor.

Urgency of first drink.

Increasing dependence on alcohol.
Feelings of guilt about drinking.

Unable to discuss problem.

Promises and resolutions fail repeatedly.

Grandiose and aggressive behavior.

MIDDLE STAGES

Increased memory blackouts.
Tremors and early morning drinks.

Complete dishonesty.

Loss of other interests.

Efforts to control drinking fail repeatedly.

Family and friends avoided.

Loss of job.

Radical deterioration of family relationships.

Physical deterioration.

Moral deterioration.

Family, work and money problems.

Neglect of food.

Drinking alone (secretly).

Begins to think responsibilities interfere with drinking.

Unreasonable resentments.

"Water-wagon" attempts fail.

Loss of willpower.

LATE STAGES

Urgent need for morning drink.

Sanitarium or hospitalization.

Persistent remorse.

Loss of family.

Decrease in alcoholic tolerance.

Hospital/sanitarium.

Unable to initiate action.

Obsession with drinking.

Complete abandonment.

"Squirrel cage".

Drinking away hangovers in vicious circles.

Onset of lengthy drunks.

Geographical escape attempts.

Impaired thinking.

Drinking with inferiors.

Successive lengthy drunks.

Indefinable fears.

Unable to work.

All alibis exhausted.

RECOVERY FROM ALCOHOLISM

Sobriety continues.
Full appreciation of
spiritual values.

Improved peace of mind.

Begin contentment
in sobriety.
Increased interest in
activity in therapy.

Confidence of employer begins.

Rationalization recognized.
First steps towards economic stability.

Appreciation of real values.

Increase of emotional control.

Rebirth of ideas.

Adjustment to family needs.

New interests develop.

New circle of friends.

New future faced with
determination and courage.

New set of moral values start unfolding.

Desire to escape passes.
Some self-esteem returns.

Natural rest and sleep.

Family and friends appreciate efforts.

Diminishing fears and anxieties.

Beginning of realistic thinking.

Application of spiritual values begins.

Regular nourishment taken.

Belief that new life is possible.

Desire for group therapy grows.

Dawn of new hope.

Spiritual needs examined.

Attempts at honest thinking.

Care of personal appearance/hygiene begins.

Told alcoholism can be arrested.

Starts to react to group therapy.

Desire for alcohol persists.

Attempts to stop drinking.

Express desire for help.

Learns alcoholism is a disease.

Drying out/medical help.

Meet recovered, normal, happy alcoholics.

BEGIN RECOVERY
(Calls for Help)

holism into (a) early, (b) middle, and (c) late stages. His work has been synthesized into "The Jellenik Chart." It will be useful to look at this chart as a comparison for diagnosing early, middle, and late stages of religious addiction.

The danger with using any general chart to describe alcoholism, which has been described in A.A. literature as "cunning, baffling, and powerful," is that it can be manipulated, twisted or used to show that a person is not addicted. After reading this chart for the first time, people are apt to make remarks like:

"These things have never happened to me...
therefore I'm not alcoholic."

"I never lost my job...
therefore I'm not alcoholic."

"My family is still with me and I've never been in a hospital...therefore I'm not alcoholic."

"When drinking affects my work or family, I'll quit...but I'm not alcoholic."

What needs to be understood is that the chart is a guide, a map, to a progressive disease, one that has symptoms and characteristics that can be recognized by those who are willing to remove the "blinders." Because no two people are exactly the same, each having varying tolerance levels, these symptoms will manifest themselves differently. The progressive deterioration described on the chart cannot be absolute. Some interpretation and imagination will be necessary to gain a "general insight" into the disease.

This is also true for religious addiction. Little information has been collected or studied concerning the religious addict, but the symptoms of this destructive disease are to be seen not only across the nation but around the world. Using the Jellenik Chart as a model, I have developed a similar chart for religious addiction.

Continuing the comparison between religious addiction and alcoholism, it is important to remember that in both addictions, the whole person is affected. Alcoholism (and indeed all the other compulsive and obsessive behaviors that have been identified from our understanding of alcoholism) is described as a "spiritual disease." Alcoholism attacks the essential nature of man, affecting self-esteem, conscience, ego, dignity, pride and hope. Alcoholism attacks relationships, especially in the family, creating anger, mistrust, shame, guilt and fear. Alcoholism attacks creative work and employment, destroying the social fabric of ordinary living. In this sense, everything and everybody is affected.

These statements are also true for religious addiction. It becomes the supreme disease because it uses the "things" of God - religion, holy writings, worship and the clergy - in a negative and destructive way, insidiously destroying man and society by employing the tools of religion. Reminiscent of the phrase, "the devil can quote scripture" - so can the religious addict! Religious addiction keeps man isolated from his spiritual nature, creating anger, fear, division and confusion. The religious addict abuses and manipulates religion, that ancient discipline that has traditionally been used in man's search for Truth, creating wars, discrimination, hatred, judgments and social unrest.

DISEASE OF RELIGIOUS ADDICTION
Progression

EARLY STAGES

Ordinary religious or spiritual life-style.

Excessive church going/ Bible study.

Going to church and using Bible to avoid problems.

Compulsively thinking or quoting scripture.

Preoccupation with church/ Bible.

Using Bible/church to calm nerves.

Praying before attending functions.

Church/Bible focus of attention. Thinking black-and-white.

Forgetting other things/engagements/ missing family gatherings.

Thinking only of church.

Loss of control phase.

Rationalization begins.

Increased use of church/Bible to avoid problems.

Secret irritation when church doctrine/ Bible readings are discussed or criticized.

Lying about church attendance/ hiding Bible.

MIDDLE STAGES

Thinking world/body evil. Sneaking attendance at church, reading Bible.

Church attendance bolstered by excuses.

Sexuality is perceived as dirty.

Obsessive praying, church going, crusades, proselytizing. Excessive financial contributions/titheing.

Messages "from" God.

Increasing dependence on religion.

Feel guilt when missing church functions.

Loss of other interests. Excessive fasting/eating disorder.

Efforts to control church going/ Bible reading fail.

Isolate from people.

Family or friends judged or avoided.

Refuse to discuss/question/think or doubt. Unable to discuss problems.

Brainwashing: family and friends.

Grandiose and aggressive behavior.

Conflict with school/work/college.

Money problems.

Secret church going.

LATE STAGES

Loss of job. Radical deterioration of relationships.

Physical & mental deterioration.

Possibly seek therapy.

Loss of family. Psychiatric assistance.

Unable to make decisions.

Obsession with church/religion.

Complete abandonment.

Continued deterioration; results in isolation, insanity, suicide.

Thinks responsibilities are conflicting with discipleship.

Unreasonable resentments.

Powerlessness.

Lengthy crusades/ mission work/communes.

Geographical moves.

Trances/stares.

Isolation with church.

Alibis exhausted.

RECOVERY FROM RELIGIOUS ADDICTION

Life gets better
& better.

Confidence in family/friends
Have peace of mind

Appreciation of
spiritual values.

Rationalization recognized.
First steps towards economic stability.

Begin contentment in freedom
and self-acceptance.

Increase of emotional control.

Increased interest in therapy.

Adjustment of family need.

Appreciation of real values.

New circle of friends.

Rebirth of ideas.
New interests develop.

New set of moral values begin unfolding.

Face future courageously.

Natural rest and sleep.

Decrease of escape anxieties.

Diminishing fears and anxieties.

Self-esteem returns.

Application of spiritual values.

Family/friends appreciate efforts.

Belief that new life is possible.

Begin realistic thinking.

Regular nourishment taken.

Dawn of new hope.

Spiritual needs examined.

Attempts at honest thinking.

Begin listening to others consider
God's uses in the world.

Told religious addiction can be
arrested.

Begin to grow in group therapy.

Desire for religion persists.

Attempts to stop religious addiction.
Learn religious addiction is a disease.

Express desire for help.

Meet normal, happy, recovering spiritual people
in Fundamentalists Anonymous.

Hospitalization (for
nerves, emotional
breakdown)

BEGIN RECOVERY
(Calls for Help)

Referring again to the Jimmy Swaggart scandal, it is interesting to note what William Martin, a sociologist at Rice University, said concerning the religious thought pattern of Jimmy Swaggart (*People*, March 7, 1988):

I thought (Swaggart) was one of the most honest and sincere preachers I had ever met. But I've seen him change over the years. He really seems to have been seduced by the power and the fame.

I think what happens to this kind of person is that he begins to think, "I couldn't have come this far if not for God." Then he begins to say, "Well, if I have this idea to build a Bible college or a mission, it must have come from God." Next he starts to say, "God told me this. God told me that..." And the next step from there is that he says, "I think what God meant to say was..."

Religious addiction keeps men chained in superstition, in ignorance and in hypocrisy.

With this understanding of religious addiction, we can perhaps understand more clearly why Karl Marx condemned religion in Russia as "the opium of the people," making the comparison between what he thought was an inept, corrupt and "spirit-less" religious system with a most dangerous drug, opium. He believed that people could become addicted around a concept of God, thus developing a restrictive belief system that was abusive and kept them slaves.

Remaining with the comparison between alcoholism and religious addiction, the following diagrams clearly show how the whole person (the spiritual being) is affected by this compulsive dysfunction.

In the diagram that follows, we see the compulsion of religious addiction. The catastrophic and long term effects on the family will be discussed in Chapter 3.

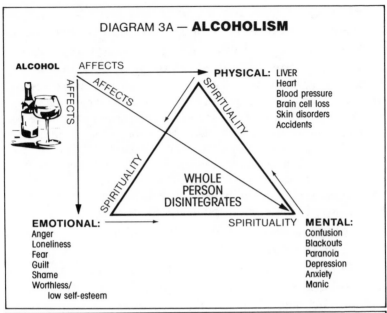

DIAGRAM 3A — **ALCOHOLISM**

ALCOHOL
AFFECTS
AFFECTS
AFFECTS
SPIRITUALITY
SPIRITUALITY
SPIRITUALITY

PHYSICAL: LIVER
Heart
Blood pressure
Brain cell loss
Skin disorders
Accidents

WHOLE
PERSON
DISINTEGRATES

EMOTIONAL:
Anger
Loneliness
Fear
Guilt
Shame
Worthless/
low self-esteem

MENTAL:
Confusion
Blackouts
Paranoia
Depression
Anxiety
Manic

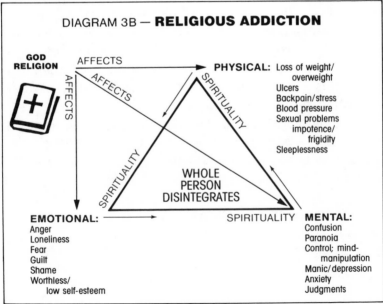

DIAGRAM 3B — **RELIGIOUS ADDICTION**

GOD RELIGION
AFFECTS
AFFECTS
AFFECTS
SPIRITUALITY
SPIRITUALITY
SPIRITUALITY

PHYSICAL: Loss of weight/
overweight
Ulcers
Backpain/stress
Blood pressure
Sexual problems
impotence/
frigidity
Sleeplessness

WHOLE
PERSON
DISINTEGRATES

EMOTIONAL:
Anger
Loneliness
Fear
Guilt
Shame
Worthless/
low self-esteem

MENTAL:
Confusion
Paranoia
Control; mind-
manipulation
Manic/depression
Anxiety
Judgments

Let us now consider some of the symptoms of religious addiction.

THE SYMPTOMS

1) Thinking only in terms of black and white - simplistic thinking.
2) Obsessive praying, going to church, attending missions or crusades, talking about God, quoting Scripture.
3) Neglecting world news, forgetting engagements and missing or avoiding family gatherings.
4) Thinking the world and our physical bodies are evil.
5) Refusing to think, doubt or question.
6) Belief that sex is "dirty."
7) Excessive fasting and compulsive overeating.
8) Unrealistic financial contributions.
9) Excessive judgmental attitudes.
10) Being brainwashed and attempting to brainwash; developing mind control.
11) Isolation from others.
12) Attitudes of conflict with science/hospitals/schools.
13) Becoming physically sick (back pains, sleeplessness, headaches).
14) Receiving strange messages from God or angels.
15) Staring - going into a trance.
16) Dramatic personality changes.
17) Unrealistic fears - the "disease cycle" of guilt, remorse and shame.
18) Family dysfunction - the breakdown of family relationships.

19) Geographical moves.
20) Cries for help; physical and mental breakdown; hospitalization.

EXPLANATION OF SYMPTOMS

1) *Thinking only in terms of black and white - simplistic thinking*

This is part of the fantasy and arrogance that dominates the thinking of religious addicts. In their lives, they see no gray areas. Something is either objectively right or wrong. This decision is usually based upon a particular and narrow interpretation of scripture. Lifestyles are seen either as "sinful" or "virtuous." Our behavior is either inspired by God or the devil.

Unfortunately, or perhaps fortunately, life is not black or white. Most religions, including the majority of Christian denominations, allow for some interpretation of scripture. The result is an ethical philosophy that is based upon a person's own particular situation. Lying is considered a sin, but there can be mitigating circumstances; for example, if you told a lie to protect some Jews from the Nazis.

Few doubt that the Bible is the inspired word of God, but we also know that it was written by men who were restricted by the social, religious and educational (scientific) thinking of their day. Jesus never wrote anything down and the incidents of His life were recorded years after His death. We do not need to be students of the "oral tradition" to appreciate that probably many incidents were left out (hence the different stories found in the four gospels) and also are dependent on the writer's subjective understanding of the situation. Some scholars consider that a variety of incidents were recorded in the gospels out of context, while other statements were remembered vaguely after the passing of time. Other stories never were intended to be taken literally - but it is not always clear what is history and what is ''story.''

For the religious addict, however, there can be no literary criticism of scripture, no debate. Because the religious addict's behavior revolves around a church, God's message as recorded in the Bible, a TV evangelist or a guru's teaching - the message must always be crystal clear: black and white.

The disciple who was taught in this autocratic manner eventually becomes the teacher - and the disease is passed on.

2) *Obsessive praying, going to church, attending missions or crusades, compulsively talking about God, quoting scripture.*

A key to understanding any compulsive or obsessive behavior is the absence of balance.

As an example, there is nothing wrong with having an alcoholic drink but, for the alcoholic, balance is replaced by craving. For most people, having a cake or cup of ice cream is not abusive or dangerous, but for the compulsive overeater, such foods (chemicals) can trigger an eating binge that could last for weeks, ending in disaster. For the addict, balance is a word that they can spell, but not understand.

So it is with the religious addict. There is nothing wrong with praying, going to church, missions, crusades or talking about God - but all of these actions can also be taken to dangerous extremes of abuse. Religious activities need to be placed within the framework of a living situation that makes an allowance for personal responsibility. To be compulsive about any of the above, to the detriment of family, friends and employment is, in a very real sense, a neglect of discipleship. A religious faith should not exist in isolation from personal responsibilities and social concerns. To have a religious lifestyle that hurts or financially embarrasses one's wife, children or friends could be considered (depending on the circumstances) selfish and abusive.

Lack of balance is the key to addiction. To talk about God is important, but we should allow others to talk, too! Indeed, if it is true that God works through His creation, then perhaps in the dialogue we will hear the creative message.

3) *Neglecting world news, forgetting engagements and missing or avoiding family gatherings.*

The religious addict is consumed by religion. Nothing else in the world seems to matter. All reading, entertainment and social events revolve around a church or mission; the result is a narrow world, a restrictive outlook and a dysfunctional Biblical lifestyle.

In the past, hobbies may have brought great pleasure and consolation; now they are ignored. Music, movies and friends are neglected. Work projects and dinner engagements are often forgotten and the nuclear family abandoned, if they are not involved in the religious addict's activities.

Religious texts are used and manipulated to justify such behavior:

Men will hand over their own brothers to be put to death, and fathers will do the same to their children; children will turn against their parents and have them put to death. (Matt. 10:21)

And everyone who has left houses or brothers or sisters or father or mother or children or fields for my sake, will receive a hundred times more and will be given eternal life. (Matt. 19:29)

So if your hand makes you lose your faith, cut it off! It is better for you to enter life without a hand than to keep both hands and go off to hell, to the fire that never goes out. And if your foot makes you lose your faith, cut it off! It is better for you to enter life without a foot than to keep both feet and be thrown into hell. And if your eye makes you lose your faith, take it out! It is better to enter the Kingdom of God with only one eye than to keep both eyes and be thrown into hell. (Mark 9:43-47)

Many scholars of the New Testament will tell you that the rabbinic style of teaching was to make extreme statements to provoke thought; to push a truth to the extreme in order to create a reaction. In a similar way, Jesus was confronting his disciples, society, the world. But it is an abuse, an injustice, to take his teachings and interpret them literally. He was not expecting his disciples or future generations to chop off their hands or pull out their eyes; rather, Jesus was presenting a challenging message that would easily be remembered.

4) *Thinking the world and our physical bodies are evil.*
A characteristic of many religious addicts is the belief that the world, our bodies and people are inherently evil. Therefore, it is necessary to "purify" themselves from contamination or cut themselves off, creating a separate and distinct remnant. The Holy Spirit is usually seen as the agent that divides, sanctifies and washes away all uncleanliness, creating a chosen people.

BREAKING THE CHAINS

Naturally, not everyone who does not believe or accept the concept of "the chosen" belongs to Satan. Ayatollah Khomeini has declared that America is Satan's Empire - the Shiites alone being specially blessed by Allah. Here are a number of his outrageous quotations.

The United States is the Great Satan from which all the little Satans of the world spring.[4]

If the religious leaders had been in power, they would not have allowed the Iranian nation to become the captive of the Americans and the British. They would not have allowed the Iranian economy to be degraded and foreign goods to be imported without customs duties....They would not have allowed the parliament to be degraded to its present state....They would not have allowed boys and girls to embarrass one another and call it dancing.... They would not have allowed males and females to go to school together....They would not have allowed innocent girls to be placed under the hands of men teachers in schools....They would have punched the government in the mouth....They would have prevented the American experts from taking advantage of us.[5]

The people of Iran have reached a state where they have attracted the attention of the world. We have gained prestige in the world, from America to the Arabic countries. This is a miracle. I think it is a spiritual one. The hands of God are with you. If it wasn't the hand of God, the nation - from children to the elderly - would not have joined our campaign. Victory is near. Don't be afraid. The Prophet Muhammad spent most of his life struggling. Learn from the Prophet and be patient. He fought all his life to overcome oppression. And we have been doing it only a short time. But what are we afraid of? If we are killed, we will go to Heaven. And if we kill, we will go to Heaven. This is the logic of Islam because we are in the right.[6]

Why should we be afraid?...We consider martyrdom a great honor.[7]

Extreme physical flagellation is often part of the purifying process, with fasting, physical punishments and praying (not sleeping) for days. Regardless of the method, the madness is the same - viewing the body and physical universe as evil and seeking to liberate the "spirit" by numerous penances and exercises. Naturally, any human being who succumbs to such treatment, especially if accompanied by sermons, quotations from holy scripture and "mind orientation" over a period of months, could be easily brainwashed.

Many cults teach and propulgate that the world and our bodies are the property of the devil. To get high or spaced - in the sense of getting away from our physical bodies and natural environment - would be encouraged. Often, drugs are used to attain a transcendental state. Remembering what we have said about the compulsive personality and the fact that many religious addicts had previously been associated with an addiction to drugs, the use of marijuana, hashish or hallucinogenics in a commune or religious sect would be attractive.

Many contemporary writings encourage the use of drugs and hallucinations as a means of experiencing relaxation or achieving a spiritual state, suggesting a progressive "enlightenment" as a result of certain chemical usage.

Carlos Castaneda...had seen it all from the inside under the guidance of Don Juan, a Yaqui Indian sorcerer. Through his successive books...Castaneda became the darling of the drug culture, turning thousands on to the benefits of mescaline. He made it all sound so appealing, this magical world that one could enter through hallucinogens, where the god Mescalito and other pagan deities were waiting to bestow incredible psychic powers upon initiates.

BREAKING THE CHAINS

In *The Second Ring of Power,* Castaneda finally makes it clear...that his Indian tutors, Don Juan and Don Genario, were really "toltec devils." Mescalito is only one of many masks Satan wears...Unfortunately, most of his readers have followed Castaneda too eagerly and too far to be able to turn back now. They are...hooked into the occult.[8]

In their book, *Chocolate to Morphine*, Andrew Weil, M.D., and Winifred Rosen offered this insight into the use of chemicals to enhance a state of consciousness:

Throughout history, people have used drug-induced states to transcend their sense of separateness and feel more at one with nature, God, and the supernatural. Marijuana was used for this purpose in ancient India, and many psychedelic plants are still used today by Indians in North and South America. Alcohol has been used for religious purposes in many parts of the world; the role of wine in Roman Catholic and Judaic rites persist, as an example. Among primitive people, psychoactive plants often are considered sacred - gifts from gods and spirits to unite people with the higher realms.[9]

In *The Natural Mind*, Andrew Weil, M.D., issued this statement:

I hope that religious organizations in this country will begin to understand that highs triggered by drugs may be more relevant to spiritual development than appearances of spirituality on Sunday mornings. If religious leaders disapprove of the use of drugs by young people, then they, of all Americans, had better look to their own mystic traditions for information on alternative methods to reach the same states of consciousness.[10]

5) *Refusing to think, doubt or question.*

These symptoms are to be closely associated with brainwashing and mind-set control. Addiction has for centuries been considered a form of slavery. People become victims, often by the ignorant and destructive choices that they make concerning their use/abuse of substances or relationships. In the case of religious addiction, this occurs when they hand over responsibility for their lives, beliefs, finances, families, employment, or destiny to a "master" or clergyman. Victims are usually told not to think, doubt, or question - as a sign of faith - and they become religious slaves. Feelings are suppressed, creativity is destroyed, choice abrogated and the adventure of life lost. Zombies, a term often used to describe drug addicts, are created.

6) *Belief that sex is dirty*.

Because the religious addict sees the physical world and our bodies as inherently evil (see symptom 4), then it follows that sex for the religious addict would often be presented as dirty. It is thought to be pandering to our lesser emotions, acceptable only in the strict confines of marriage and then only for procreation, not pleasure. Historically, the Roman Catholic Church has, because of traditional statements from the early fathers, reflected the attitude that celibacy and virginity were "higher" spiritual states than regular marriage.

St. Jerome, who had spent years in the Ethiopian desert dressed in sackcloth and fasting for a week at a time to banish visions of bevies of dancing girls, declared, "He who too ardently loves his own wife is an adulterer." His position became Church doctrine; laymen must settle for the lesser state of marriage.[11]

He (St. Augustine) took the writings of Paul and opened by chance to the words, "Not in reveling and drunkenness, not in lust and wantonness, not in quarrels and rivalries. Rather, arm yourself with the Lord Jesus Christ; spend no more thought on nature and nature's appetites."...Augustine's writings show acute fear of losing conscious controls. To him...the mindless tempest of orgasm, the most uncontrolled of states, was farthest from God.[12]

(Augustine) called celibacy the most blessed state; but physical celibacy is meaningless when the mind is full of desire, so constant self-policing is needed. Marriage is a rung on the ladder to salvation, but a lower one than chastity...They should couple for procreation, not for pleasure (sinful).[13]

(Thomas) Aquinas' (doctrine) became unshakable law for the faithful: sex, even in marriage, shows a degree of moral abasement; the ideal state is freedom from impulse; the deepest and most dangerous impulse is sex.[14]

The impression is that God had created sex, and then had second thoughts about it!

Even the natural bodily functions were associated with sin; menstruation was described as "the curse," connecting it with the sin of Eve. A young man's "wet dreams" (emissions) were seen as a sign of dirty thoughts, resulting in punishment if the stains were discovered. Sexual intercourse, followed by withdrawal, or an induced act of masturbation were considered a serious sin and many young men were told that such an act could lead to blindness or insanity.

The story of Onan was described in Genesis (Gen. 38:9-10):

And Onan knew that the seed should not be his; and it came to pass, when he went unto his brother's wife, that he spilled it on the ground, lest that he should give seed to his brother. And the thing which he did displeased the Lord: wherefore he slew him (also).

Homosexuality, for the religious addict, would almost certainly be seen as a deadly sin, too terrible to talk about or discuss. Anybody who was judged to be homosexual would normally be expelled from the congregation unless he repented and asked for forgiveness. Such an attitude would create tremendous guilt and shame for the religious addict who at times experienced homosexual feelings or was a "closeted" homosexual. Here we see the conflict that leads to homophobia. In my book, *Spirituality and Recovery*, I explained homophobia in the following way:

The disease of homophobia is fed by hate and prejudice. The long-term goals are divisive and destructive. Homophobia often masks feelings of inferiority and loneliness, reflecting personal pain and self-hatred. As with the disease of addiction, the dynamics need to be understood. The homophobic needs to be loved and understood and gently led to self-acceptance and integration.

Many males afflicted with homophobia pretend to be "real men." They build up muscles, swagger around the streets, look theatrically strong and tough, act "macho" and dress accordingly.

Another form of homophobia involves the W.A.S.P. (White Angle-Saxon Protestant) look. Neat, clean and ever-so-dull! Ties and office shirts are mandatory, even on vacation. Gray is their favorite color. Red is avoided like poison. A tense, controlled outlook on life is revealed, even when you ask to borrow the garden spade. Incidentally, the garage, garden and workroom are always in order. To be caught with a dirty car would be like dropping your pants in public: embarrassing, humiliating, and human.

Many homophobics discover a "high" and "buzz" in hating. Hating gays and Communists. The two are often irrationally connected. Homophobics avoid looking too deeply at themselves. Like all drug users, they manipulate the hate and prejudice to escape. They are in pain but too proud to ask for help. The pain is the basis of their disease.[15]

7) *Excessive fasting and compulsive overeating*.

The keys to understanding this symptom are the words "excessive" and "compulsive." Moderation is not only absent but impossible until the addiction is admitted and counseling begins. In some cases, the fasting is a symptom of another dysfunctional disorder, anorexia nervosa. It may have been progressing over the years, and "finding religion" becomes an excuse to continue the disorder under the camouflage of holiness. It is possible that the excessive fasting developed around the religious addict's display of devotion could also trigger anorexia nervosa. Whatever the "why" or the "how," the result is a dangerous abuse of the body, one that affects health, personal relationships and productivity at work or school. Again, when the body is physically drained and takes on the induced state of trance that often follows long periods of fasting, that individual is particularly susceptible to brainwashing or "mind control" messages.

Compulsive eating (bulimia) is another common disorder among religious addicts. So many religious addicts were brought up in a family system that was religiously restrictive. The rules were no smoking, no drinking, no dancing, no playing cards, or relationships with the opposite sex until an announced engagement, etc. The one thing you were allowed to do, and were encouraged to do, was eat. And so behind the food, beneath the fat, lay the buried feelings of anger, resentment, guilt, shame, confusion, and hypocrisy. The fat became a wall that the religious addict hid behind from the world; isolated from a society that he condemned yet hardly knew; angry at the joy, excitement and vitality that he saw in a people who "did not have the Lord" and yet were happy. The religious addict exhibits a pious rage!

8) *Unrealistic financial contributions.*

This is the symptom that has been examined recently by the media in the Jim and Tammy Bakker, Oral

Roberts and other TV evangelists sagas. In spite of the scandals and extravagancies, the money continued to pour in. Many disciples explained or excused their financial contributions by saying to reporters that they were not sending money to the TV evangelist, but rather to the ministry, or God's church or the work of the missions. However, reality reminds us that God does not put the money in the bank or decide how much money to send to the missions, schools or hospitals in Africa. That is the work of the board members! We know from the extravagancies at the P.T.L. that corruption and abuse were prevalent.

Time Magazine reported:

Increasingly, a growing number of Americans are focusing on the doings of the huge, semisecret gospel business empires like PTL that have sprung up in little more than a decade of fervent television preaching. Many are not happy with what they see. A Gallup poll survey this spring showed that since 1980 there has been a sharp decline in American public esteem for four of the country's most important TV preachers: Oklahoma-based Oral Roberts (whose approval rating dropped from 66% to 28%), Swaggart (76% to 44%), Virginia's Pat Robertson (65% to 50%), and California's Robert Schuller (78% to 61%).[16]

In the same story, Jim Bakker is reported as saying:

Even if Jim and Tammy did everything we're accused of, does that give Jerry Falwell the right to steal my dream, my life, my home, my everything and my reputation from me?[17]

Strange, I thought the ministry belonged to God!

With the disease of religious addiction, everybody seems to pay and nobody wins. The religious addict believes he is contributing to Jesus, God's church, the mission of healing, because that is what the TV evangelists tell the viewers: "You are giving to Jesus" - but the reality is a sophisticated financial network.

BREAKING THE CHAINS

Across the nation, guilt and shame buttons are pressed in a thousand different ways and people pay "the tithe" to comfort their consciences. Often, the sick are promised healing and forgiveness in exchange for generous contributions. The sales techniques that are employed and keep contributions flooding in are applauded by advertisers and yet many of those giving are the old, the sick, the lonely, and the addicted.

After years of working in the field of addiction, it is not uncommon to hear the stories of families being left destitute because alcoholics, drug addicts, compulsive credit-card users had spent their life savings - now we must add to this list the families of religious addicts.

9) *Excessive judgmental attitudes*.

Perhaps one of the most dangerous, destructive and disturbing aspects of religious addiction for a multi-religious society is the arrogant judgment made against people who do not share the same beliefs. Depending on the religious addict's faith, Jews, Muslims, agnostics, Catholics, evangelicals, fundamentalists, Buddhists and a variety of liberal thinkers are dismissed as heretics, pagans or doomed sinners. This produces fear, anger, violence, shame and guilt in the majority of people living in this country. People fear to ask questions; many are ignorant of the background and historical development of other religions. Television and radio have tended to avoid airing critical discussion programs about religion. Religious zealots command the air waves. A nation is divided and millions are condemned or made to feel guilty, all in the name of God.

Biblical texts, twisted history, tradition, and incomplete or biased research are used to bolster arguments that support the various judgments. Religious addicts become modern-day "storm-troopers." The God of Love is presented as the Eternal Judge; many who were made to kneel before the "wagging finger" learn to point the finger at others.

The writing is on the wall for all who are prepared to look. Wars, persecutions, and countless deaths over the centuries have resulted from zealous religious groups (comprised of many religious addicts). Excessive judgments are directed towards those whose only crime is being different. Variety, comprehensiveness is anathema to the religious addict.

10) *Being brainwashed and attempting to brainwash; developing mind-control.*

The control that many religious leaders or TV evangelists have over a congregation or viewing audience is maintained by restricting criticism, doubt or debate. Their message is: Don't think—accept; don't reason—obey. The argument is presented that "the leader" has been appointed or chosen by God to deliver "the message," and a faithful disciple is one who unquestioningly follows. The test of faith is seen in the disciple's willingness to serve the various commandments - regardless of family, friends or reason.

Many religious addicts were brought up by a father, mother or grandparent who controlled and directed their belief system. As children, if they did anything that broke the rules, they were to confess it and receive the punishment. If they used slang or offensive words, the offending children must wash out their mouths with soap. Failure to go to church, falling asleep in the sermon or forgetting a studied scriptural text resulted in a beating. Feelings of anger, fear, and "difference" were instilled in the child. This religious brainwashing would contribute to the dynamics of religious addiction or religious abuse, and, if left untreated, would be passed on to the next generation.

11) *Isolation from people*.

All addicts isolate. Their attitude, behavior, lifestyle eventually conflict with moderate behavior and they separate to avoid criticism and protect their denial system. Alcoholics, in the second-stage of addiction, will avoid spending evenings with social drinkers. They drink to drink and not to socialize.

Religious addicts are the same. Their religious addiction demands that they spend time with people who think, talk, pray and worship as they do - except when they are out proselytizing.

This isolation can be self-induced or the product of organized mind-control. "Babies" or "newly converted" need to be removed from any influences that might create doubt or criticism concerning the message. They are placed in a separate community (commune) or distinct group requiring special clothes, symbols, and worship buzz-words. They must be surrounded by people who believe the same things.

Many young people are attracted to this apparent asceticism. They find meaning and security in the clothes, symbols, and autocratic assertions. In a world that is often confusing, these young people have found something definite. They are made to feel special, members of the chosen, the elite. Also, the insecure, abandoned and lonely will find in many of these groups a family atmosphere they have longed for; those running from an emotional problem will discover a place to hide. Religious addiction flourishes among the immature, those who have low self-esteem, and those who have felt abandoned.

12) *Attitudes of Conflict with schools/hospitals/ science*.

Many religious addicts, because they are narrow and restrictive about what they think or believe, often have conflicts with medicine and education. Frequently we read about a father or mother who refuse to give permission for a doctor to perform an operation or carry out a blood transfusion - producing dire consequences for the child.

The Jehovah's Witnesses is a religious denomination that often disagrees with science, education and medical treatment. Here is a list of printed guidelines that they distribute to the faithful with scriptural references.

Bible is God's word and is truth -

All Scripture is inspired by God and is useful for teaching the truth, rebuking error, correcting faults, and giving instruction for right living, so that the person who serves God may be fully qualified and equipped to do every kind of good deed. 2 Tim. 3:16-17. Also, 2 Peter 1:20-21, John 17:17.

Christ was first of God's creatures -

Christ is the visible likeness of the invisible God. He is the first-born Son, superior to all created things. Col. 1:15. Also, Rev. 3:14.

Earth will never be destroyed or depopulated -

There he built his Temple, like his home in heaven; he made it firm like the earth itself, secure for all time. Ps. 78:69. Also, Eccl. 1:4

There is only one road to life -

There is one body, and one spirit, just as there is one hope to which God has called you. There is one Lord, one faith, one baptism. Eph. 4:4-5. Also, Matt. 7:13-14.

Only a little flock of 144,000 go to heaven and rule with Christ -

Then I looked, and there was the Lamb standing on Mount Zion; with him were 144,000 people who have his name and his Father's name written on their foreheads. And I heard a voice from heaven that sounded like a roaring waterfall, like a loud peal of thunder. It sounded like the music made by musicians playing their harps. The 144,000 people stood before the throne, the four living creatures, and the elders; they were singing a new song, which only they could learn. Of all mankind they are the only ones who have been redeemed. Rev. 14:1-3. Also, Luke 12:32, Rev. 5:9-10.

Satan is invisible ruler of world -

We know that we belong to God, even though the whole world is under the rule of the Evil One. 1 John 5;19. Also, 2 Cor. 4:4, John 12:31.

A Christian must have no part in interfaith movements -

Do not try to work together as equals with unbelievers for it cannot be done. How can right and wrong be partners? How can light and darkness live together? How can Christ and the Devil agree? What does a believer have in common with an unbeliever? How can God's temple come to terms with pagan idols? For we are the temple of the living God! As God himself has said,

"I will make my home with my people and live among them; I will be their God, and they shall be my people."

And so the Lord says,

"You must leave them and separate yourselves from them. Have nothing to do with what is unclean, and I will accept you." 2 Cor. 6:14-17. Also, 2 Cor. 11:13-15, Deut. 7:1-5.

A Christian must keep separate from the world -

Do not love the world or anything that belongs to the world. If you love the world, you do not love the Father. 1 John 2:15. Also James 4:4, John 15:19.

Taking blood into body through mouth or veins violates God's laws -

The Holy Spirit and we have agreed not to put any other burden on you besides these necessary rules: eat no food that has been offered to idols; eat no blood; eat no animal that has been strangled; and keep yourselves from sexual immorality. You will do well if you take care not to do these things. With our best wishes. Acts 15:28-29. Also, Gen. 9:3-4.

Man did not evolve but was created -

So God created human beings, making them to be like himself. He created them male and female. Gen. 1:27. Also, Isa. 45:12.

To place faith in any doctor rather than the miraculous power of the Spirit is blasphemy. Family members, acting out their co-dependency, unknowingly support and enable the religious addict. A similar problem is seen when the religious addict interacts with schools or educational centers. Science is acceptable, so long as it does not conflict with Bible stories or scriptural statements; naturally, conflicts abound.

13) *Becoming physically sick (sleeplessness, back pain, headaches).*

As we saw in the earlier diagrams (page 52), the human being is comprised of the mental, emotional and physical. They all interact.

Religious addicts, like any other compulsive and obsessive person, have emotional, physical and mental stress as a result of their addiction. The fear, anxieties and internal conflicts that plague religious addicts often create psychosomatic disorders. When they consult doctors, the religious addiction is rarely perceived or discussed, resulting in continued physical sickness.

This is also true for the co-dependent (family). People often escape the religious addict with a physical complaint, staying in bed for weeks at a time to avoid the stress, arguments, put downs and conflict caused by religious addiction. It's impossible to calculate how many young children have developed a physical sickness as a cry for help from their parent's or grandparent's continued religious brainwashing.

14) *Receiving strange messages from God or angels*.

It is difficult to argue with a message that comes from God or one of His angels! Part of the denial system or control is the use and manipulation of divine messages. Extraordinary behavior, unrealistic demands, and excessive judgments are excused with such statements as:

> "God told me to do this...to say this...to condemn those who are..."

> "The Spirit guided me in this decision."

> "Christ came to me last night and said..."

I believe that God is involved in this world and He uses certain individuals as messengers. It is important, however, that we consider these messages in the context of previous revelations, Biblical statements, scientific research and tradition. We must not restrict God's activity to religion. God is at work in this world and He speaks through artists, scientists, psychologists, and everyday commom sense. Healthy criticism is essential in all aspects of education and it needs to be applied to "messages from God." Many people who are recovering from a psychiatric disorder have, at one time, claimed that they had received messages from God. Today they are thankful that people did not believe or act on their instructions.

15) *Staring - going into a trance.*
Many drug addicts develop a strange appearance under the influence of drugs; they look "spaced" or "high," developing a pale pallor, glassy eyes and a fixed stare. This is occasionally seen in the religious addict.
Mother Nature often assists our intuitive perception of sickness by causing people to look like what they in fact are; people appear healthy, energetic, happy, depressed or sad.

The religious addict often looks sick, appearing in a trance and oblivious to what is going on around him. I appreciate that a trance-like state often accompanies a person after meditation or spiritual exercises. It also can reveal a compulsive disorder (rather like an alcoholic's blackout) when the person's physically there and yet "absent." If we see in the religious person this "spaced" affect in the home, at work or in a variety of situations where involvement is expected and necessary, then we might be witnessing an advanced religious addiction.

16) *Dramatic personality change.*
A characteristic of any drug use is a precipitative per-

sonality change. Drugs and chemicals are taken because they "do" something and, over a period of time, addicts experience exaggerated mood swings. Persons become excessively "hyper" when they are on the drug or very depressed and lethargic when they are coming down.

Religious addiction is also a disease that affects the personality: people become excessively happy, joyous, loving, enthusiastic and positive when they are "in the Spirit." They will spend nights singing hymns and chants, discussing the scriptures, praising and fasting, telling family and friends how they came to "see the Light" and became "reborn." But then follow long periods of cynicism, anger and severe judgments toward the "ungodly" or those unimpressed and critical of their conversion story.

Also, after a long time "in religion," a period of self-doubt, guilt, and depression can develop because:

(a) they see the flaws and inconsistencies in "the master," the group or sect. Or they are no longer convinced by the scriptural explanations - and yet they are afraid to express the doubts that disturb them.

(b) Sometimes, they feel they are not true disciples, either because of a lack of faith or because they are consumed by impure thoughts. Their personality is affected by the anger and resentment they feel for their personal failure.

As with other addictions, it is this change of personality that concerns family and friends, indicating that something is wrong. Family and friends make statements like:

He stays in his room night after night, eating very little; he just reads the Bible and stares at the crucifix.

She looks physically sick. Her complexion is white, she is thin and appears lacking in energy. She never talks to anybody. Occasionally, she will get excited when she is going to a crusade, but then returns with depression and self-doubt. She has no friends.

When he first got into religion, he talked about it all the time and upset many people because of his emphatic judgments and arrogance; he appeared too perfect to live! Today he avoids family members, has none of his old college friends calling and spends all his time at the Mission or in a Bible study group. He looks intense, manic and tired. He never seems to rest, always in a hurry - I'm worried about him.

She had a good job and was going to school in the evenings. Then, out of the blue, she gave up the job and said she was going to work for a Christian commune for $300 a month. No discussion, no explanation, no questions! She sold her condo and gave the proceeds to the church. She never calls her parents, does not reply to the letters and cannot leave the commune without permission from the "elders." Is she happy? We doubt that very much because if she was, why would she need to be protected, kept as a prisoner - with no television, radio, or newspapers. She is not the girl we used to know!

All the above statements I have heard from concerned, angry and distressed parents or friends. As with other addictions, the disease is progressive, affecting the whole person, producing dysfunctional relationships with those who do not share the same belief system - and it is apparent.

17) *Unrealistic fears - "disease cycle" of guilt, remorse and shame.*

The advanced stages of religious addiction has all the

fear and paranoia found in other chemical dependencies and compulsive behaviors. The system of delusion that seems to work for a time becomes progressively destructive. Many religious addicts reach a stage where they make the following statements:

(1) Everybody is against me or talking about me,
(2) God is angry with me,
(3) I need to get my "message" to the world,
(4) The devil is coming after me,
(5) The family has joined forces with Satan to destroy my ministry and discipleship,
(6) People are trying to kill me,
(7) Nobody understands me,
(8) The world is coming to an end,
(9) I have lusted in my heart and I'm full of remorse and guilt,
(10) The Lord is asking for a sign of my commitment; I must leave family, job and financial security and offer myself for the Lord's ministry.

Such statements indicate an emotional crisis. As we have already seen, many religious addicts, before they found religion or were "reborn," have already received treatment for emotional anxiety or chemical dependency. They have a fear of being "put away" that conflicts with their need to "declare the message." Irregular eating, sleeplessness, geographical moves, anger tantrums, long periods of silence, bouts of depression - all accompany these fears. *A critical and dangerous stage has been reached in the disease process*.

It is important to see how these fears, together with the guilt, remorse, and shame, create the vicious cycle that we see in all aspects of addictive behavior. The alcoholic's drinking creates the stress, isolation, and low self-esteem and yet it is believed that only alcohol will ease the pain.

The gambler is in debt and yet he continues to think that if only he can win the jackpot, all his debts can be paid off. The vicious cycle of addiction!

So it is with religious addiction. The danger is that when the feelings of fear, guilt, and remorse develop, the religious addict creates in his life the "vicious cycle" that takes him back into the autocratic religion that *produced* these feelings. He is incapable of seeing a way out of his addictive cycle without help. His helplessness makes him vulnerable and dependent, following the dictates of any religious priest, minister, rabbi, or mullah who offers instant forgiveness and inner peace for the price of total dedication, unquestioning loyalty and blind faith. This vicious cycle continues because the religious addict sees no alternatives or options.

18) *Family dysfunction - the breakdown of family relationships.*

The disease of religious addiction is a family disease, a relational disease. It produces discomfort, anger, isolation, fear, guilt, low self-esteem and shame also in the family members. You cannot have a religious addict that you love or care for and not be affected. You cannot live in the same house with a religious addict and not be affected. We have learned in treating drug addiction that addicts affect those around them.

In the next chapter, we will see how the religious addict affects the family, and use the insights into family dysfunction we have gained from our study of other compulsive and obsessive disorders.

19) *Geographical moves.*

We observe geographical moves accompanying the later stages of religious addiction. The reasons and excuses are numerous, and only indicate the denial process, the need to escape, to avoid the responsibilities of their behavior. The following are some examples:

> "People do not understand me. Nobody in the home believes me. I need to get away to hear what God is saying to me."

> "The Master says I can do whatever I want with my life. I need to start my life over again in another city."

> "Jesus told me to leave everything and follow Him. I am determined to live out of my discipleship and move away."

> "My family and friends do not "believe" and judgment will surely fall upon them. I am going to live with my new 'Christian' family in the commune."

> "I love my family but I am called to serve the world. I shall go and live in the Mission House. My wife and family can choose to come with me or stay at home."

As we have seen with other addictions, the geographical moves can be manipulated to create and continue the "victim role":

> "I have hurt too many people. I cannot face my family or friends, so I am going away to a place where I am not known."

> "I am angry that my religious obsession destroyed my marriage, my job, . . . everything. I want to go away and hide in shame."

We know that geographical moves can be very dangerous. Once you start to run from problems you create a behavior pattern that is hard to break. It is better to stay and face the consequences, to make amends and seek support from people who understand. It was the feelings of low self-esteem and not being good enough that helped to create the religious addiction. Therefore, the solution is in building up confidence, dignity, and personal self-worth. Escaping through geographical moves is not the answer. Once the religious addict realizes that God is not going to "fix him," then he can begin the task of fixing himself, where he is!

20) *Cries for help; physical and mental breakdown; hospitalization.*
The religious addict has reached rock bottom. The family does not know what to do. Friends recommend a therapist or psychiatrist and often the religious addict spends time in a psychiatric unit. On rare occasions, a chemical dependency treatment center is considered for help. An intervention is requested from somebody in A.A. or another self-help group (i.e., Fundamentalists Anonymous).

The tragedy is that few people recognize or understand the symptoms of religious addiction. It is the purpose of this book to create an awareness and discussion of religious addiction and religious abuse so that it can be treated alongside other obsessive and compulsive disorders.

FOOTNOTES

1. "Hospitalization of Patients with Alcoholism." *Journal of the American Medical Association*. October 20, 1956. p. 750.
2. Bissell, Dr. Le Clair and Paul W. Haberman, *Alcoholism in the Professions*. (New York, Oxford University Press, 1984) p. 90-92.
3. *Alcoholics Anonymous*. (New York, A.A. World Services, 1976) p. 30-31.
4. McManus, Doyle, "Cast of Political Players in Iran." *Los Angeles Times,* January 27, 1981. Part 1, p. C.
5. "The Ayatullah's Hit Parade," *Time,* V. 113, (February 12, 1979) p. 37.
6. Ibid.
7. "Angry Attacks on America." *Time,* V. 114, (December 3, 1979) p. 24.
8. Hunt, Dave, *The Cult Explosion*. (Irvine, California, Harvest House, 1980) p. 37-38.
9. Weil, M.D., Andrew and Winifred Rosen, *Chocolate to Morphine*. (Boston, Houghton Mifflin Company, 1983) p. 16-17.
10. Weil, M.D., Andrew, *The Natural Mind*. (Boston, Houghton Mifflin Company, 1972) p. 199.
11. Karlen, Arno, *Sexuality and Homosexuality*. (New York, W.W. Norton and Company, 1976). p. 72.
12. Ibid, p. 75.
13. Ibid, p. 76.
14. Ibid, p. 77.
15. Booth, Fr. Leo, *Spirituality and Recovery - Walking on Water*. (Pompano Beach, Health Communications, 1985) p. 93-94.
16. Brand, David. "God and Money." *Time,* V. 130. (August 3, 1987) p. 49.
17. Ibid.

Chapter 3

THE FAMILY

We know that the disease of addiction affects the family. We know that it affects relationships with relatives, co-workers, friends and spouses. In this sense, addiction is a relational disease.

Co-dependency is concerned with explaining how spouses, the family, and other relationships are affected. How do the children from addicted families take their childhood experiences into adulthood? What happens emotionally to them? Let us look again at some recent interpretations of co-dependency:

Robert Subby, in his book *Co-dependency: An Emerging Issue*, says:

An emotional, psychological, and behavioral condition that develops as a result of an individual's prolonged exposure to, and practice of, a set of oppressive rules - rules which prevent the open expression of feeling as well as the direct discussion of personal and interpersonal problems.[1]

Marie Schutt says:

It's the process of one person standing between an alcoholic and the crisis caused by the spouse's drinking. It's a protective stance adopted by the spouse that keeps the husband from experiencing the consequences of his drinking.[2]

Dr. Judi Hollis says:

A co-dependent under/overeater is someone whose life is intertwined with the person who has an eating disorder. Their mission in life is to cure the food abuse. They forget their own lives to help another.[3]

Judi Hollis later adds:

. . .someone who is addicted to another's addiction.[4]

Co-dependent behavior is also involved in religious addiction. The family of the religious addict is affected. The family members either take on the belief system that the father (or mother) brings into the home, resigning to "put up with it," or they rebel. But they are certainly affected.

Because God is involved, because the Bible is said to be the basis of the lifestyle, because "righteousness" is the goal and "heaven" the reward, it becomes progressively more difficult to object and not get involved. It is hard to rebel against God! Religious addiction manipulates through the "guilt-trip." Who wants to argue with the Bible? Who is not for God? How can anyone object to a "godly" message and lifestyle? Messages learned in childhood are revamped and refined; yesterday's "guilt-buttons" are pressed. Unlike the chronic anti-social behavior of the alcoholic and drug addict, it is difficult to know when discipleship deteriorates into addiction. When does devotion develop into an obsession with fantasy? How can reading and teaching the Bible be seen as an abuse of the family?

It is important to understand that, with a religious addict, we are not talking about Christian discipleship, or any other kind of "spiritual behavior" - we are talking about addiction. Although we use the word "religious," the dynamic of the disease creates the opposite of a true relationship with God. Indeed, religious addiction is an abuse of God. As with chemical dependency, religious addiction involves using God, the Bible and people in a negative and destructive way. It is the lack of balance that produces the addiction and abuse.

Many women who have been married to religious addicts, who have been abused for years by "the preaching spouse," will be able to identify with Marie Schutt's description of an alcoholic wife:

> The alcoholic has a tremendous ability to transfer the guilt he feels onto those who love him. His wife usually is the most eager recipient, because she already feels emotions that conflict with her values of a rewarding family system. She has been angry, sulking, silent, and screaming - all to no avail.
>
> The co-dependent wife is eager to believe she is in control. She will attempt to have everything perfect in the home. She tries desperately to be a perfect wife and a perfect mother, and she conveys a sense of tense perfection to her children. Her unspoken thoughts: "If only I make our life as perfect as possible, His Drinking will vanish."
>
> But since her behavior is not the real cause of His Drinking, all of her attempts to make him quit drinking end in dismal failure. The consequences? Frustration and guilt. Whatever she does, it isn't enough, it doesn't have any impact on His Drinking.
>
> The co-dependent wife finds herself in a no-win situation, "damned if she does and damned if she doesn't." Many wives of alcoholics refer to this behavior as "walking on eggshells" when he is around.[5]

The co-dependent begins to doubt herself. She thinks something is wrong with her. It is her problem. Perhaps she needs to see a doctor! And the more she isolates, builds a wall around her questions and feelings, the more confused and helpless she becomes. As she cooperates with the religious obsession, she becomes more co-dependent (dysfunctional). And always there is the nagging question, "Who would understand?"

Let us examine the dynamics of co-dependency when applied to the spouse of the religious addict. Referring again to Marie Schutt's book, *Wives of Alcoholics*, we can apply some of the rules of the care-taker co-dependent to the religious addict:

(a) Peace at any price
(b) Maintain the conspiracy of silence
(c) Never quit
(d) Never discuss feelings
(e) Try to seem normal.

(a) *Peace at any price*

The wife of the religious addict does not want to cause any arguments or any upset in the family; she does not wish to appear to be the nagging wife or seek to emphasize actions that she knows to be "a little odd" or "strange." Remember, certainly for the woman with a Christian background, religion has given a definite message concerning her conduct:

> Wives, submit yourselves to your husbands as to the Lord. For a husband has authority over his wife just as Christ has authority over the church; and Christ is himself the Savior of the church, his body. And so wives must submit themselves completely to their husbands just as the church submits itself to Christ. (Eph. 5:22-24)

> I also want the women to be modest and sensible about their clothes and to dress properly; not with fancy hairstyles or with gold ornaments or pearls or expensive dresses, but with good deeds, as is proper for women who claim to be religious. Women should learn in silence and all humility. I do not allow them to teach or to have authority over men; they must keep quiet. For Adam was created first, and then Eve. And it was not Adam who was deceived; it was the woman who was deceived and broke God's law. But a woman will be saved through having children, if she perseveres in faith and love and holiness, with modesty. (1 Tim. 2:9-15)

These messages have been around for centuries. They are part of the culture of a society. It is almost impossible to separate them from our attitude in worship, education, politics, law, literature, and social behavior. Only slowly are women being emancipated from the subservient status created for them by historical religions.

Now if these rules and directions have caused confusion and debate among "ordinary" religious folk, they have created dramatic reactions from religious addicts and abusers! The religious addict continues to use Biblical texts and tradition to maintain yesterday's status quo. Any relaxation in tradition is seen as the work of "liberals" and "communists." The purity of God's word is used to keep the women (and the entire family) in their religious places. Recently, a brutalized co-dependent wife of a religious addict shared:

> I truly believe that my husband was attracted to this extreme fundamentalist church because of what it said about women and the place of women in the home. I was constantly told I was "inferior," secondary. I was to obey him. Physical abuse was excused by scriptural texts. And for years I believed I was a bad person!

By remaining silent, millions of spouses of the religiously addicted develop an emotional sickness that cries out for treatment. As with alcoholism, the disease of religious addiction progresses and it is only a matter of time before the judgments and condemnations that were directed toward an ungodly society become directed at the frightened and passive family. *Eventually, nothing that the family does is good enough*!

(b) *Maintain the conspiracy of silence*

The religiously addicted family dies in the "lie of silence." We have seen in treating other addictions that "doing nothing" is, indeed, "doing something." But that something is enabling the family system to become more dysfunctional to the point of disintegration. Religious addiction progresses until it affects everything!

BREAKING THE CHAINS

The world, foreign governments, nations, society, school systems, and the arts are judged according to the religious addict's narrow interpretation of the Bible. People are ostracized because of lifestyle. People are judged because of their religious beliefs. To doubt, ask questions or think - depending on the conclusion - could be seen as blasphemy. Dancing, smoking, drinking and non-religious television viewing are seen as corrupting and sinful. Perfection, holiness and purity become impossible burdens; guilt, shame and gloom overshadow the household of the religious addict. Yet nobody says anything!

In many homes where religion is abused, we see a hypocritical lifestyle. The yearning for physical, mental and spiritual perfection is often followed by bouts of anger, violence and sexual abuse, followed by guilt, remorse and self-pity. Again nothing is said.

The religious addict may disappear for weeks, the family not knowing where he has gone. Has he gone on a crusade? Has he returned to his "womanizing" past? Has he gambled away the savings? The fear and anxiety is written all over the wife's face as she seeks to comfort the family - but nothing is said.

When the fine line is crossed between discipleship and obsession, when balance is lost, when compulsive behavior concerning a religion is apparent to everybody - trances, weird visions, prayers that go on through the night, hearing angelic voices conveying "strange" messages, termination of employment due to religious posturing, unrealistic financial contributions being made to a T.V. ministry - and still nothing is said, this is the conspiracy of silence. And the tragedy is that silence does not work. The enabling family only creates more pain. It is this silence that will eventually create the dysfunction, even in the children.

It was the silence that was so maddening. Everybody knew that the Biblical texts were selected as an excuse for the weekly punishments. I knew he enjoyed giving us a "whipping" but he read from the scriptures to make it okay. And my mother knew it. I think I am more angry at her because she knew he enjoyed it and yet she said nothing. (Tom, age 42)

I think my mother knew he sexually abused me. I was fourteen years old and my father was still watching me shower and bathe - insisting that he dry me with the towel. That is not normal! Always the touching. Always the caressing. And nothing said. Everything done in silence. (Barbara, age 26)

If I did not go to mass I could not eat that day. The family sat around the table and I was alone in the corner. If I missed confession, I could not eat with the family. Nobody spoke to me. Nobody was allowed to comfort me. All this was done in the name of God! It was the silence that hurt; it is the silence that I remember. (Paul, age 28)

A woman, who eventually divorced herself from her religiously addicted husband, shared with me her guilt and shame concerning her silence:

For no reason, he would hit the boys. He said they were arrogant and badly behaved. He accused them of sexual misconduct, indecency and taking the Lord's name in vain. When they tried to answer back, he beat them - followed by a time of prayer! And I remained silent. For years I remained silent.

In the bedroom, he made me do things to him and then said it was sinful. What he said the boys were thinking, he did with me in bed. He transferred his feelings onto the boys and when he punished them, he was punishing himself. And I remained silent.

Even today I cannot talk to the boys about it. We have never talked about it. (Mary, age 62)

BREAKING THE CHAINS

(c) *Never quit*

There is something about the wife (or husband) of the religious addict that makes them "hang in." They never give up, hoping that things will be "miraculously" changed. They are not believing in miracle - but magic! Perhaps because of their dysfunctional background, they see miracle as something God does - they have no understanding of cooperation, or of our involvement and participation in the miracle by the risks we take in life. The wife obeys the husband in the same way that she would obey God, no discussion. This is partly because of the brainwashing, "mind-set control," or narrow interpretation of texts like:

> . . . The law rules over people only as long as they live. A married woman, for example, is bound by the law to her husband as long as he lives; but if he dies then she is free from the law that bound her to him. (Romans 7:1-2)

This "never-quit" mentality keeps religious co-dependents victims; martyrs who keep the misery alive in their homes. God is thought to have created the events, temptations and conditions that we must live with; this is how He "tests" us. The wife might even believe that her marriage is the "cross" she must carry. This is a variation on the popular belief concerning death: "If your name is on the bullet, you will get it." There is no emphasis on freedom, choice and personal responsibility; rather, there is a convenient and irresponsible form of predestination that creates apathy, passivity and helplessness. Such an attitude discounts human spirit, determinism and change. The "never quit" attitude allows people to wallow in the martyr/victim role.

The spouses and family members of the religious addict pray that God will do something. In the silence of their prayers, they beg for help. They know something is wrong; they sense that the God of Love would not condone such cruel abuses or intemperate judgments - but they never quit.

Surrender is a key word in recovery from chemical dependency and it is portrayed as a powerful insight to change. In my book, *Spirituality and Recovery*, I wrote concerning surrender:

Surrender follows "the moment" you open your eyes to the real you. Really see the dynamics of a disease in your life, recognize obsessive behavior, catch the insanity in your life.

Is your marriage working?
  Are you drinking too much?
    Is your gambling causing problems?
      How many cigarettes are you smoking, and can you breathe in the morning?
        Do you eat too much?
          IS YOUR RELIGION A MEANS OF AVOIDING LIFE?
            Are you sick and in need of help?

Surrender to the reality of your life. Put aside the fancy talk and lies. Be real. Surrender.[6]

To never quit is suicide!

(d) *Never discuss feelings*

The religious addict and family co-dependents do not discuss feelings because the message is:

Everything is perfect.

BREAKING THE CHAINS

Our faith in God has removed earthly problems.

We are the chosen people and God will help us.

Criticism is not acceptable, especially if it pertains to the Bible, minister or directed religious lifestyle. As with co-dependents to other addicts, the religiously abused family stuff their feelings behind their beliefs. Remember, the addicted family is living in a world of fantasy, unreality - "spaced" is a good adjective. They are not living in the real world. They do not face the world the way it is, but rather how they want it to be. They dismiss as irrelevant the problems that their religious outlook cannot solve. Emotions are often considered a sign of weakness. Everything is "fine" and "okay."

As with alcoholism, drug addiction, eating disorders and the menu of compulsive and obsessive disorders that are rife in our society, the family of the religious addict develops, reflects and imitates the dysfunctional symptoms that we find in the religious addict. Let us look at the symptoms of religious addiction and abuse again and see the connection with the progressive family dysfunction, remembering that these symptoms are lived out within the family system.

1) Thinking only in terms of black and white.

2) Obsessive praying, going to church, attending missions or crusades, talking about God or quoting scripture.

3) Neglecting world news, forgetting engagements and missing family gatherings.

4) Thinking of the world and our physical bodies as evil.

5) Never talking, doubting or questioning.

6) Thinking that sex is "dirty."

7) Excessive fasting and compulsive overeating.

8) Unrealistic financial contributions.

9) Excessive judgments.

10) Being brainwashed and brainwashing; developing "mind-control."

11) Isolation from others.

12) Conflicts with science/hospitals/schools.

13) Becoming physically sick (back pains, sleeplessness, headaches).

14) Receiving strange messages from God or angels.

15) Staring - going into a trance.

16) Dramatic personality change.

17) Unrealistic fears - the "disease cycle" of guilt, remorse and shame.

18) Family dysfunction - breakdown of family relationships.

19) Geographical moves.

20) Cries for help: physical and mental breakdown: hospitalization.

We are discovering that there are a variety of addictions within the family of the addict. Naturally, the religious addict will desire to get his spouse and family involved in their religious practices, and a number succeed. Many wives and husbands of religious addicts have told me that they became as obsessive and compulsive around the Bible, God, ritual, or T.V. evangelist as their addicted partner. That is consistent with the studies of wives and husbands of alcoholics who say, "If you can't beat them, join them." They escape from painful confrontations by joining the circus! Brainwashing and mind-control are used on family members, and they can be effective.

Alternately, many spouses of the religious addict seek solace in other chemicals - in alcohol, prescription drugs, cigarettes or food. Little research has been done concerning the family of the religious addict, but my suspicion is that many religious co-dependents hide behind food. My image is of the well-dressed religious addict being followed by a woman who is submissive, controlling, defensive, protective and overweight!

When Judi Hollis describes the co-dependent in *Fat is a Family Affair*, she is also describing the religious co-dependent:

In describing a *confluent* personality type, we refer to people who have no sense of their own ego boundaries. In other words, it is hard for them to know where they stop and another person begins. Everyone seems to ebb and flow into each other. "When you have a splinter, my finger hurts." This quality of being perceptive and aware of the other person, the ability to walk in another's shoes, is often an asset. Such confluence makes many terrific actors and actresses, nurses, doctors, and psychologists. As a co-dependent, your confluence also helps in dangerous situations, as you develop a healthy caution. You can deftly sense what is going on in the other person. In families, however, this confluence leads into a tangled web where you lose your own identity in the service of others. In addictive families, members become so enmeshed in each other's needs and identities that it takes extensive work to get untangled. Each family member will have to learn how to speak for him - or herself and develop separateness. You may think you know what your loved one is thinking long before they say it. Often you may be right, but assuming you've got them figured out is actually disrespectful. You rob them of the chance to be surprised and learn something new about your relationship. Recovery is a whole new ball game.

It is safe to say that a codependent is *someone who is addicted to another's addiction.*[7]

The feelings that are stuffed in the religiously ad-dicted/abused family are:

anger,
  guilt,
    shame,
      self-pity,
        helplessness,
          frustration,
            low self-esteem,
            loneliness,
              confusion,
                desperation.

(e) *Try to appear normal.*

Remember the co-dependents in the religiously addicted family have an investment in being seen as "normal." The family of God should not be seen as having problems. They all love each other, they are always happy. The children all go to school and get good grades. The house is clean all the time; relatives and friends are always coming to stay. They have no "habits" hazardous to their health (i.e., drinking, smoking, or staying out late); the wife is seen to be affectionate towards her husband and children; the husband is seen to "take care and take charge"; the children's friends come from "good" families. Alcoholism and drug addiction does not occur in this family!

All this is too good to be true, and we know it is not "real" - this is the illusion that necessitates the secrets. Slogans are used to perpetuate this illusion:

The family that prays together, stays together.

God takes care of His own.

Cleanliness is next to Godliness.

Prosperity and health are the inheritance of the righteous.

Indeed it is the stress and strain of trying to appear "perfectly" normal that produces the need for the other symptoms of co-dependency:

(a) Peace at any price.
(b) Maintain the conspiracy of silence.
(c) Never quit.
(d) Never discuss feelings.

For the religiously addicted family, any failure, imperfection or scandal is seen as a disgrace to God, to the church, the ministry, or the preacher. The religious addict and abused family produce a co-dependency that extends beyond the family into society, beyond society into the world; it extends beyond the world into the universe. It would not be too extreme to suggest that the religiously addicted family eventually becomes co-dependent around God. What a burden to carry through life!

FOOTNOTES

1. Subby, Robert, *Co-dependency, An Emerging Issue.* (Hollywood, Fla., Health Communications, Inc., 1984) p. 26.
2. Schutt, Marie, *Wives of Alcoholics: From Co-dependency to Recovery.* (Pompano Beach, Fla., Health Communications, Inc., 1985) p. 2.
3. Hollis, Ph.D., Judi, *Fat Is A Family Affair.* (Minneapolis, Minn., Hazelden Foundation, 1985) p. 38.
4. Ibid, p. 39.
5. Schutt, Marie, *Wives of Alcoholics: From Co-dependency to Recovery.* (Pompano Beach, Fla., Health Communications, Inc., 1985) p. 7.
6. Booth, Fr. Leo, *Spirituality and Recovery.* (Pompano Beach, Fla., Health Communications, Inc., 1985) p. 74.
7. Hollis, Ph.D., Judi, *Fat Is A Family Affair.* (Minneapolis, Minn., Hazelden Foundation, 1985) p. 39.

Chapter 4

ADULT CHILDREN ISSUES

The religious addict affects the family and this certainly includes the children. As with children from other dysfunctional family systems, the children in the religiously addicted home were made to feel different from other children. They looked like other children, occasionally tried to play games like other children, sat in school with other children - but they did not *feel* like the other children. They felt "different," more serious, more rigid, more responsible: little adults in children's clothing. Why? Because of all the "don'ts" they heard:

"Don't play with those children."

"Don't listen to that music."

"Don't wear those clothes."

"Don't play those games."

"Don't say those words."

"Don't touch that part of your body."

"Don't read those books."

"Don't eat that food."

"Don't question the Bible."

"Don't separate yourself from God."

"Don't speak against your parents."

The religiously abused children become dysfunctional and take on roles that have been identified in the chemically dependent family. Sharon Wegscheider-Cruse in her book *Another Chance,* has identified the following roles:

BREAKING THE CHAINS

1) Hero
2) Scapegoat
3) Lost Child
4) Family Mascot.

1) *Hero:* This child seeks to gain love, attention and bring stability into the family by being "exceptional." If only he (or she) could do better, then the arguments, the punishments, the financial problems, the "abandoned moments" would go away. The "hero" grows up goal oriented - he must succeed in everything he does; he must win the prize.

The Hero is helpful inside the family circle and successful outside. He provides those moments of hope and pride that even the most desperate families experience from time to time, furnishing a source of worth for the family when all other sources have run dry. Indeed, the Hero sometimes seems "to have it made," to be so "together" that he bears no scars of the emotional strife at home. But his facade of good nature and success is an illusion. Behind it, he, too, feels miserable. Ironically, his very success may make him the most difficult member of the family to reach with treatment.[1]

Because of the religious training and "brainwashing" that this child had received over the years, he would naturally be the child who would take his hopes and fears to God, with excessive devotion. This child in adulthood could easily become addicted to religion or reject everything (because of its apparent failure), and develop an emotional dependency on alcohol or drugs.

2) *Scapegoat:* This child is forever being blamed, accused of horrendous sins, punished and made to feel "bad." He feels that whatever goes wrong in the family is his fault. Nothing he can do is "right" or "good

enough." While his brothers and sisters are often praised, he is ignored or given the message, "Why can't you be like the other members of the family?"

This child might "act out" in school, Sunday school or become rebellious at home or in society.

Because of his own bottled-up emotions, the Scapegoat finds himself attracted to other youngsters who are acting out their frustrations. He begins by merely getting into mischief, but the trouble-making escalates. He starts using alcohol or other drugs heavily. Before long he finds himself involved in a car accident, expelled from school, or picked up by the police for vandalism, shoplifting, or some other charge.[2]

He can never do "good" - so why try? In later life, sex, violence, alcohol, drugs, cigarettes, and food might be used to act out his rebelliousness.

The guilt and shame messages that "the scapegoat" was barraged with in childhood could create serious self-esteem problems in later life. He (or she) might carry so much guilt into adulthood that he seeks to make up by marrying a "good Christian woman" - and the cycle continues.

It is this child who often recants stories of physical, emotional and sexual abuse.

3) *Lost Child:* This child sees the problem in the family, but is unable to verbalize what he sees. He does not try to compete with the "Hero" or the "scapegoat" - his solution is to "get lost" in the family system. Because his presence is absent in the family, little interest is taken in his work, clothes, hobbies, or friends. He creates a fantasy world of his own, usually through reading books or playing solitary games; if he has a pet or soft toy it will become his special friend or family. Although

his social skills do not develop, his imagination knows no boundaries. At school the lost child does not do well because he is unable to create meaningful relationships.

Sharon Wegscheider-Cruse says:

> During the first several years of developing my model of the alcoholic family roles, I considered the Lost Child a Scapegoat who just happened to manifest his sense of rejection by the family in a particular way. But I have since realized that there are fundamental differences in the two roles. True, both children find themselves locked out of the original triangle of parents and Hero, but their responses to that primal frustration are at opposite poles - a difference that will reverberate through all their responses to the recurring challenges of life.
>
> Emotionally, both rejected youngsters suffer from low self-worth. However, the Scapegoat's is a slowly growing self-hate, rooted in unfavorable comparisons to the Hero and in his own anti-social behavior; the Lost Child's lack of self-worth simply results from years of being ignored and treated as though he did not exist. The Scapegoat, feeling unfairly excluded from the heart of the family, is hurt and angry; the Lost Child, on the other hand, accepts his exclusion as all he deserves, experiencing loneliness and worthlessness, but little anger.[3]

We can see that the Lost Child is a natural for religious addiction. He might get lost in Biblical stories, have visions of the Virgin Mary and angels, create in his mind a "special" relationship with the Lord, compensating for his feelings of worthlessness by being "chosen." I wonder how many modern-day Elmer Gantrys were, in their households, the "lost child?"

(d) *Family Mascot:* This child sees the anger, frustration, craziness and delusion of the religiously addicted family; he feels the loneliness, confusion, and isolation that the other members of the family experience - but he compensates by "creating a scene." As a child he learned that tears bring attention, that noisy behavior got him noticed; if he could make the family laugh, then he was popular.

The Mascot, who creates fun wherever he goes, has some things in common with the Hero. Both manage to get positive attention for themselves and at the same time bring good feelings to the family. When the other members of the family laugh at him, it relieves their tensions, too. Everyone seems to forget, at least for a moment, how grim it all is. Mascots, however, also vent their hyperactivity in annoying habits and bursts of sudden, erratic behavior, so the attention they receive can be negative as well as positive.

Whether entertaining or merely agitated, the Mascot's behavior *achieves* its purposes: it puts him in control of the family scene for as long as he can hold the floor and so makes him feel more secure; it brings him attention of some kind, whether positive or negative; it moves family members to some rare honest expressions of feeling, whether laughter or scolding; and it temporarily takes the spotlight off the Dependent and the family crisis.

You do not have to be with a family more than a few minutes to know which child is playing this part. He may act cute and helpless, or show off, or joke around and refuse to take anything seriously, or squirm and interrupt and do "crazy" things. He may beguile you, but he is very hard to ignore.[4]

If the Mascot were to stay in religion, he could easily become a minister or priest! This child grew up to be the charmer, the joker, developing a means of communication that would place him as a leader of the pack, possibly a T.V. evangelist - and yet the deep-seated feeling of abandonment would always be just below the surface. Indeed, it is those feelings of being unloved that generate the clown, the joker - perhaps generate the ministry!

I have also met many alcoholic types who fit this character. Remembering past conversations in bars, after the sixth drink, and between numerous jokes, they share how they grew up in a "very religious home," strict and disciplined, everything forbidden except prayer and worship; they never felt loved. They were never held or hugged, never played ball with their father like the other kids - and so they created "a circus." And many years later, they are still playing that same tragic character.

It cannot be emphasized enough that the children from a religiously addicted family can "play" more than one of the above roles; at different times in their lives they might catch themselves playing both "the hero" and "scapegoat" - but always feeling the "lost child."

Once these roles are realized, many of the children from religiously addicted families find meaning and identification in the numerous ACoA (Adult Children of Alcoholics) meetings across the country - discussing feelings that have been buried for years.

Buried Feelings:

anger	uncomfortability
worthlessness	dirty
isolation	threatened
confusion	condemned
desperation	competitive
trapped	helpless
guilty	defensive
shame	evasive

These feelings did not exist in isolation; they affected behavior at school, in the playground, at college, among friends - as well as in the home. The real tragedy for the children in religiously addicted homes (as we have seen in chemically dependent families) is that a combination of exaggerated feelings arise from conflicting, confusing and unhealthy messages. These messages are:

> you are different,
>> chosen,
>>> special,
>>>> blessed,
>>>>> forgiven,
>>>>>> redeemed--but you are also fallen,
>>>>>>> sinful,
>>>>>>>> dirty,
>>>>>>>>> evil,
>>>>>>>>>> helpless.

As in the alcoholic home, the element of inconsistency reigns supreme. The father could be loving one moment and violent the next. In the night, mother's voice is heard screaming from the bedroom, but in the morning not a word is spoken. God was perfect Love and yet He was feared because of the horrible punishments He dealt out. Always inconsistencies.

As with children of alcoholics, so the children of religious addicts take their dysfunction, their hurt and abused feelings into adulthood.

Janet G. Woititz, in her book, *Adult Children of Alcoholics*, gives some characteristics of the adult child that, with some adaptation, fits for the Adult Children of Religious Addicts.

1. Adult children of religious addicts guess at what normal is.

BREAKING THE CHAINS

Adult children of religious addicts come from a family that is compulsive and obsessive about all the "don'ts" concerning God, the Bible and a church. Also if there were a number of other "addictions" within the family system (i.e. workaholism, eating disorders, prescription drug abuse), if fear was the dominant feeling they learned and remembered concerning their childhood, if they grew up with guilt and shame and their family never showed loving feelings - how could they be expected to know what normal is? They were given the message, in various ways, that they were "different" - normalcy would be beyond their comprehension.

2. Adult children of religious addicts have trouble following a project through to the end.

Nothing they did was ever good enough. They were always trying to be "perfect," trying to be what God, the preacher, the church, father or mother wanted from them, but it was never enough.

They remembered that when they were praised, it was followed by:

. . . and next time you can do even better.

. . . however, do not get too proud because it is really God, not you, doing this.

Often they were told directly that they were no good, not good enough, a sinner like all the rest, and that without God or the Holy Spirit, they would never be anything. And throughout their childhood they believed this. Their self-esteem was close to the dust! As a result of this nurturing, they often felt that they had failed before they had started. They entered the interview for a job not feeling "good enough." The attitude was, "Why bother," or "What's the use?"

3. Adult children of religious addicts lie when it would be just as easy to tell the truth.

For years they were afraid to tell the truth because they thought that they would be punished; everything was "sinful" or it was forbidden in their home. Things that other children did every day - dance, watch television, play sports, read adventure books, flirt - were not permitted in their home. Many played away from home. Then they learned to lie. Always they felt guilty and ashamed - but they lied to live. Often, when they did things that they thought were okay, they were punished.

David, a child from a religiously addicted home, explained it this way:

I was punished when I did not do anything wrong. My father said that that was for the times I did things that were sinful and he did not catch me!

We know that religious addicts, like other addicts, are temperamental, moody, and in order for their children to survive in the dysfunctional environment, it became necessary to create lies, manipulation and pretense. And this "make-believe" was taken into adulthood. Adult children of religious addicts often don't know why they lie - sometimes to impress, often just to say something, to avoid arguments or discussion or "...just because."

4. Adult children of religious addicts judge themselves without mercy.

BREAKING THE CHAINS

Remember, nothing was ever good enough. The model for living was Jesus, the Virgin Mary, the prophets and the saints! Ordinary people, ordinary living, ordinary thoughts were considered "sinful." The message was, "you are a bad person," until they were filled with the Holy Spirit. At church and in the home, they heard the same (constant) message:

Jesus died for your sins.

You are the sinner who made God put His "Only Son" on the cross.

Today Jesus is still suffering because of your sins.

The message was clear; they were not good people. God loved them - but then again, only God could love them! As the Psalmist says, "I am a worm and no man."

The Bible readings, the prayers and the services reinforced what they had learned from the cradle: "You are a bad person."

Be merciful to me, O God, because of your constant love. Because of your great mercy wipe away my sins! Wash away all my evil and make me clean from my sin! I recognize my faults; I am always conscious of my sins. I have sinned against you - only against you - and done what you consider evil. So you are right in judging me; you are justified in condemning me. I have been evil from the day I was born; from the time I was conceived, I have been sinful. (Ps. 51:1-5)

...As a sick man I approach the physician of life; as a man unclean, I come to the fountain of mercy; blind, to the light of eternal brightness; poor and needy, to the Lord of heaven and earth. I beseech You, therefore, in Your boundless mercy, to heal my sickness, to wash away my defilements, to enlighten my blindness; that I may receive the Bread of Angels, the King of kings, the Lord of lords, with such reverence and humility, such contrition and faith, such purpose and intention, as may help the salvation of my soul... [excerpt from Prayer of St. Thomas Aquinas][5]

5. Adult children of religious addicts have difficulty having fun.

Fun was a sin - or so it appeared. Life was serious. The world was a battlefield where the army of God fought with the army of Satan. They were to be soldiers, not children!

Games were forbidden. My mother was over thirty before she felt comfortable enough to bring playing cards into the home without feeling guilty. In the religiously addicted home, kissing, wrestling, football, dancing, music, magazines, theater, and "the circus" could be considered sinful.

The image of God was that of a serious, ever watchful, judgmental and angry "Old Man." His children developed the same characteristics!

The fun, joy and comfort of a meaningful sexuality was lost to millions because of messages received in childhood. The adult child of the religious addict finds it difficult to even talk about sex, let alone enjoy it. The body was sinful, therefore sex was sinful. Fun and sex were incompatible.

Arno Karlen, in his book, *Sexuality and Homosexuality*, states:

The writings of St. Augustine show an acute fear of losing conscious control through experiencing pleasure from sexual activity. To St. Augustine only the serene and rational decision-making process was the way to God. The most uncontrolled state of orgasm was the farthest from God.[6]

In the writings of Saint Paul it is noted:

> Not in reveling and drunkenness, not in lust and wantonness, not in quarrels and rivalries. Rather, arm yourself with the Lord Jesus Christ; spend no more thought on nature and nature's appetites (sex).[7]

Many Roman Catholics were severely affected by this religious teaching, especially when it was neither interpreted nor explained within the context of a historical background.

6. Adult children of religious addicts take themselves very seriously.

This goes along with not having fun. One reason it was difficult to have fun was because they took themselves too seriously. When most of the world is considered depraved, sinful, or unhealthy, then it was, indeed, a most serious existence. Redemption, eternal life was dependent upon them not getting involved with the "ways of the world." Work, study, prayer, worship and reading scripture were the ingredients of discipleship; they were the "stuff" of daily life.

A woman (Pat) who is recovering from religious addiction told me that she still feels guilty and awkward when she is in a room where people are laughing or "being silly." Pat is in her fifties and has never experienced a belly laugh or cried with laughter.

7. Adult children of religious addicts have difficulty with intimate relationships.

Adult children of religious addicts find it very hard to be intimate, share their body or their feelings when they were told from childhood that "mankind is sinful," "fallen," "depraved," or "evil." When the focus of spirituality was outside their body, their person, their humanness, how can they share or allow another person into their life? When touching, holding hands, hugging, kissing or even expressing feelings were absent in their lives, then intimate relationships become not only difficult but *scarey.* And yet they want them!

They see other people walking in the park, sharing their lives, being physical and emotional with each other and they want that for themselves - but everything in their childhood experience tells them it is "bad" or "sinful."

8. Adult children of religious addicts overreact to changes over which they have no control.

So much of religious addiction and abuse revolves around "control." Things are kept black or white, orderly, everything in its place, no questions or doubts, no confusion, a system, a "mind-set." Why? Because the edifice of religious addiction is built upon the "givenness" of God's word that is perfect and infallible. The fear is that once a piece from the house of cards is removed, then everything could come tumbling down!

If the Bible is not God's fundamental word, with no inconsistencies or inaccuracies - then perhaps literary criticism has some validity.

If the Holy Spirit is not directing the preacher or minister, then he could be wrong in his sermons or directives.

If the mullah is not "God's chosen prophet," then to blindly follow would be insanity.

If there is not only "One Way" - or one religion that has "The Truth" - then perhaps we should listen and study the religion or cultural philosophies of other peoples.

The children of religious addicts resist change, discussion or conflict because they fear that everything they have been brought up to believe, everything they spent their teenage years accepting, might not only be questioned but proved to be wrong. They isolate and stay in their "mind-set groups." Hence the inappropriate anger when a text or belief is questioned or criticized.

9. Adult children of religious addicts constantly seek approval and affirmation.

Remember the mixed messages that they have received since birth: that God loves them, they are chosen, they are specially blessed in baptism - and yet they are sinful, in need of redemption, stained by the worldliness of "original sin." Self-esteem and confidence are rooted in God, the church, other people's acceptance and approval of their lives. Their behavior is co-dependent concerning religion!

Adult children of religious addicts are unable to create or discover God in their lives. They are unable to discover God in the beauty of their physical bodies and relationships. The "image" of God was lost - it was seen only in large congregations, impressive ritual and the pomp of the church. Their value was in becoming one of those numbers - sometimes by making excessive financial contributions.

10. Adult children of religious addicts usually feel different from other people.

Of course, they feel different - all their lives they were told they were different. They were the chosen, the sanctified, the blessed, the people of God - and the people who existed outside their "sect" were the ungodly, the children of Satan.

They lived differently. Often they did not dress as their contemporaries (avoiding colors or modern designs); they had food laws and regulations; avoided dance, theater, music, and "worldly entertainment"; did not socialize with people outside their group or religion; they developed a language, culture, and worship that emphasized their differences. They not only felt different but they would tell people that they were different. Often it was this difference that made them feel special.

11. Adult children of religious addicts are super responsible or super irresponsible.

The contradictory messages that children from religiously addicted homes received makes them ambivalent concerning responsibility. On the one hand, they felt their implied "chosenness" gave them a message for the world. They felt super-responsible for family, friends, co-workers, and members of their congregation. They wanted everybody to share in the "fruits of righteousness" and they would go to any lengths to convert people to their belief system. We have all experienced the people who come to visit armed with Bibles or "holy" books. They would knock on a neighbor's door and share their testimony of the "good news." They would visit a sick person with healing oils and promises of recovery (in this life or the next!). They felt super-responsible for delivering "The Word." They were the channels of God's message, the modern prophets.

This is seen in the book *Rock Hudson, His Story,* which describes when Rock Hudson was near death:

> The next day, Sunday, the actress Susan Stafford called and said the Boones had been having a round-the-clock prayer vigil for Rock and wanted to come lay on hands. Susan had been a friend of Rock's since 1970, and was a born-again Christian and intern minister. Tom says, "I figured, they couldn't do any harm." Fifteen minutes later, the group was in Rock's bedroom, kneeling around the wooden bed with their hands on the sheet. Shirley Boone led the prayers while Rock slept.[8]

> . . . Toni Phillips, the night nurse, said to Tom, "I haven't told you this before, but I'm a member of the prayer vigil the Boones have been having, and they want to come again and pray with Rock."
>
> "Get 'em over," said Tom.
>
> Rock was unconscious, but Pat Boone placed a Bible on his chest and took his hand. Tom got in bed with Rock and held him, and Eleanor fell to the floor and began speaking in tongues.[9]

However, they could also behave in an irresponsible manner if people did not accept "their message." The text they use to justify their behavior is usually:

> And if some home or town will not welcome you or listen to you, then leave that place and shake the dust off your feet. I assure you

that on Judgment Day God will show more mercy to the people of Sodom and Gomorrah than to the people of that town. (Matt. 10:14-15)

Family members who refuse to hear "the Word" would be thrown out of the house, a son or daughter disowned, relatives and friends ignored. Often children of a religious addict, who have become as obsessive and compulsive concerning religion as their parents, will change jobs, neighborhoods, friends if they experience criticism or antagonism concerning their religious message. If the "heathen" asked for a crumb of bread, it would be denied!

Also, it should be recognized that after such dysfunctional nurturing, *many* children from religiously addictive homes reject God, religion and the church when they become adults. Their experience of being the Hero, Scapegoat, Lost Child or Mascot had been so painful that they reacted in adulthood with anger, cynicism, and irresponsible behavior. Some get involved in alcohol and drugs, many trust nobody and are unable to sustain intimate relationships. Others grow up hating the happiness experienced by others and become dangerously pathological in a variety of ways - physically, emotionally, and sexually. The tragedy is that just breaking away from their parents or religion, without help, therapy and an understanding "support group" still leaves them dysfunctional; they remain dangerous to themselves and to others.

12. Adult children of religious addicts are extremely loyal, even in the face of evidence that the loyalty is undeserved.

One of the messages that children from religiously addicted parents learned was the need to be loyal. This message also enabled the cycle of control to continue - being disloyal was seen as a sin. Incidents that happened in the family (or church) were kept within the family system; you did not talk with outsiders or strangers.

Connected with this characteristic was the manipulated use of "forgiveness." If a parent did something to hurt you - physical violence, sarcasm, sexual abuse - they would appeal to the Christian quality of "forgiveness."

Don't say anything to anybody, don't do anything to cause scandal for the family or church.

Again, the loyalty strings would be pulled!

We see an example of this in the Jim and Tammy Bakker scandal. The financially contributing members remained "loyal" in the face of mounting evidence of financial extravagances and corruption in the leadership of that church. The members invented excuses or cited mitigating circumstances to maintain their loyalty.

Observers of Evangelism predict that, in the short run at least, PTL supporters will rally around their beleaguered organization. The TV ministries like PTL occupy powerful positions because they meet the spiritual and emotional needs of millions of viewers. Indeed, loyal fans of the Bakkers reacted with surprising equanimity to the couple's disappearance.

. . . a daily viewer of religious TV, contributes upwards of $10,000 a year to televangelists. He is irritated by all the criticism of the Bakkers. "These people have done a lot of good in their lives," he says.

. . . an Idaho freight salesman, is not bothered by the lavish lifestyle that the Roberts' (Rev. Oral Roberts) and the Bakkers are said to enjoy. To him, "their rewards should be great, because they've done great things for the Lord."[10]

13. Adult children of religious addicts tend to lock themselves into a course of action without giving serious consideration to alternative behavior or possible consequences. This impulsivity leads to confusion, self-loathing, and loss of control over their environment. As a result, they spend tremendous amounts of time cleaning up the mess.

Remember, children of the religious addict were molded to think in terms of "black and white," the straight way and the crooked path, heaven or hell, the righteous and the unredeemed. To think about an "alternate way" of living was considered blasphemy, disloyal to God and His precepts.

However, the adult child of the religious addict lives in this world and he sees another way to live, while at work and on the television, in books and magazines or from friends. Occasionally he tries to live in both worlds, enjoying the worldliness of work and friendships, but also returning to the "righteousness" of home. This conflict leads to confusion, self-loathing and an eventual loss of control. Isolation, physical and mental breakdowns, drug abuse, eating disorders, sexual acting-out and violent outbursts of anger could arise - always followed by guilt, shame, and fear of God's Judgment.

Intervention, treatment, therapy, and an understanding "support group" are the only solutions to this disease that is abusing millions of children and adults who live in religiously addictive environments.

FOOTNOTES

1. Wegscheider-Cruse, Sharon, *Another Chance*. (Palo Alto, Ca., Science and Behavior Books, Inc., 1981) p. 104.
2. Ibid, p. 117.
3. Ibid, p. 131.
4. Ibid, p. 140.
5. *St. Joseph's Daily Missal and Hymnal*. (New York, New York, Catholic Book Publishing Co., 1966) p. 672.
6. Karlen, Arno, *Sexuality and Homosexuality*. (New York, W.W. Norton and Co., Inc., 1971) p. 75.
7. Ibid.
8. Hudson, Rock, and Sara Davidson, *Rock Hudson, His Story*. (New York, Avon Books, 1987) p. 320.
9. Ibid, p. 322.
10. Ostling, Richard N., "TV's Unholy Row," *Time*, April 6, 1987, p. 67.

Chapter 5

WHO IS AT RISK?

I am often asked the question, "Who is at risk?" My reply is always, "Many more than we might think."

Although I believe this statement to be true, in that the prevalence of dysfunctional religion is everywhere, there are certain groups that specifically should be mentioned.

(a) *The Compulsive*:

There is a saying that many compulsive people can identify with: "Fools rush in where angels fear to tread." The compulsive, by nature, are always rushing into things. The fact that none of us are angels and all of us are fools, at times, means that unless we have a strong and supportive recovery program and are able to catch our bouts of "craziness" and do something about them, we will experience pain and discomfort as a result of this compulsivity. As we have seen in earlier chapters, it is not too dramatic to state that we have become an addictive society. The compulsions seem endless and cut across every facet of life;

food	relationships	parenting
gambling	credit cards	caffeine
drugs	emotions	nicotine
alcohol	cults	love objects
sex	television	therapy
physical exercise	sugar	sickness
work	pain	

BREAKING THE CHAINS

Another compulsion, which is the focus of this book, is religion. We need to remember that addiction (compulsion) is fundamentally an escape mechanism, a technique for avoidance, a journey away from self. A compulsion is directed towards something outside of ourselves that we believe will make us feel good,
behave stronger,
remove the problem,
make intimacy easier,
give confidence,
create energy,
improve the world.
So we escape from reality into a world of fantasy. We seek to spatially remove ourselves from the pain (''get high'') or endeavor to move away from the discomfort (''go on a trip'').

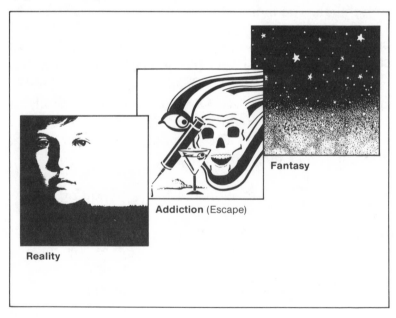

Fantasy

Addiction (Escape)

Reality

For the compulsive person, the one who is always doing something, going somewhere, completing a project, expecting a letter, too busy, in a hurry - "business" itself can become the escape, the addiction; and always they miss *themselves*.

The psalmist says, "Be still...and know that I am God."

The poet, W.H. Davies, picks up this theme and says:

> What is this life,
> if full of care,
> We have no time,
> to stand and stare.[1]

The "great lie" is that something from the outside is going to make life better. Something beyond me will make me feel good, acceptable, lovable or worthwhile.

This is true for the religious addict. The God outside of me - who is understood by others, whom I can't get close to unless I follow the teachings and separate myself from the "ungodly" - that God will "fix" my life!

Now the danger for the compulsive person is that religion itself can also become the "drug of choice." Perhaps earlier, in his teenage years, the religious addict might have sought relief in drugs, food, alcohol, sex, work...and now, at a later stage in his life, he is introduced to religion. And the cross-compulsion pattern continues. Now he uses religion, the message, the T.V. evangelist, in exactly the same way he used drugs - *and misses himself*.

Instead of using the gift of religion to understand his own specialness and dignity, the religious addict continues to beat himself up, wallowing in his sinfulness and failure. The religious addict remains a victim of the god of others and misses the creative contribution that only he can make. Instead of perceiving the "oneness" of this universe and the beauty of variety in the peoples and cultures of the world, the religious addict arrogantly escapes in condemnation, isolation, and religious divisiveness.

(b) *The Abused (Emotionally, physically, mentally, or sexually)*:

An insidious characteristic of abuse is that it gets the victims to believe at different times the following:

the abusive behavior is normal,

they deserve it,

there is nothing they can do to change it,

they must never speak about it,

someday it will all go away.

The feelings of powerlessness, the belief that nobody will understand or be able to help, keeps the victim of abuse trapped for years - tragically, for some, all their lives. In recent autobiographical publications, the subject of abuse (violence, incest, rape) has been mentioned, carrying the clear message of hope that comes with change. The change is knowing that, as human beings, we have been given power (the "spirit" of God) and it is in our struggle for self-determination that we experience dignity.

In her book, *I, Tina*, Tina Turner tells about her years of physical, emotional, mental and sexual abuse and how she broke away to become her own person.

The plane arrived at the Dallas-Fort Worth airport, and we were walking out of the gate and Ike was just staring at me - one of these real evil looks, trying to work on my mind. There was a car and driver waiting there to take us to the Hilton, and as soon as we got in, Ike hit me again - *whap!* Another one of those backhand licks. And then I started fighting back. He kept hitting me, but I didn't cry once. I was cursing him out: He was going, "Fuck you," and all of that, and I'd keep talking right back to him. He was amazed! He was punching me and saying, "You son of a bitch, you never talked to me like this!" I said, "That's right - but I am now!" And then *pow*, and he'd hit me again. And then he reached down and got his shoe off his foot and *pow, pow, pow!* But I kept fighting him. I didn't care what he did, because I was *flying* - I knew I was gone.

By the time we got to the Hilton, the left side of my face was swollen out past my ear and blood was everywhere - running out of my mouth, spattered all over my suit. Ike used his usual story; said we'd had an accident. The people at the Hilton looked at me and I could tell they were wondering how I'd ever get onstage that night looking the way I did, all beat-up and battered, with my one eye swollen almost shut. I think Ike knew, too, that this was really the end. But he'd been up so long, he was just too tired to deal with it. We went up to our room and I heard him mumble something like, "Lord have mercy" - something not typical of Ike at all - and then he went and lay face down on the bed. I didn't want him to get any ideas about what I was thinking so I acted like nothing had changed, I said, "Can I order you something to eat, Ike?" Same as always, still playing the maid. It was a little hard to get the words out this time, because my mouth was so cut and swollen, but I tried to make everything seem normal. Then I went over to the bed and started massaging him, as usual. I was afraid he would hear my heart, it was beating so loud - because I knew it was time to walk. But I kept massaging him and rubbing his head, and he soon started snoring. I slowly took my hands away, just to see if he was really asleep. I heard his deep, dead kind of snoring sound that he made after he'd been up for several days, and I knew he was out. I looked at him for a second and I thought, "You just beat me up for the last time, you sucker." Then I got up, and put a cape over my bloody clothes - didn't even change them. I had to leave my wig there because my head was too swollen to wear it, so I just tied one of these stretch straps around my head, I figured he could get somebody else to wear that wig - he could wear it himself, for all I cared. I put on a pair of sunglasses, picked up one piece of hand luggage with just some toiletry things in it, and I was gone.[2]

Earlier in her book, Tina Turner had the awareness of her "specialness" that had come from positive affirmations in a Buddhist chant. She goes on to say:

And I would think about Ike's face, and how funny it was to finally see him scared: to know at last that he wasn't all-powerful, that he wasn't God, that there was a little piece of God inside each of us - inside of me, too - and that I could find it, and it could set me free.[3]

In Norman King's book, *Everybody Loves Oprah*, the subject of Oprah Winfrey being sexually abused is discussed.

Among the relatives was a nineteen-year-old male cousin - ten years older than Oprah. Instead of going home, the cousin frequently stayed over at the apartment.

"They put me in bed with him," Oprah explained later. (Actually, the cousin was put in bed with Oprah.) "There was only one bed, and I had to sleep with him. Can you imagine? I didn't know anything about sex that summer."

One night her cousin simply took advantage of her and raped her in the bed. She was too naive - too petrified - to know what was going on, too surprised to fend off this older cousin. She was left stunned and puzzled by what had happened.

The cousin knew exactly what to do. To keep her quiet about it, he took her out to visit the zoo, and bribed her there with an ice-cream cone.

"I didn't tell anybody about it because I thought I would be blamed for it," Oprah explained.[4]

Years later, Oprah Winfrey discussed her child abuse, saying:

I was [some years older] when I did an interview with someone who had actually been sexually abused. It was the first time it occurred to me that this thing that had happened to me had also happened to other people. I hadn't told anybody until then because I thought I was the only person it ever happened to and I thought it was my fault because afterward it happened repeatedly - with different people.[5]

Anybody who has been consistently "abused" develops a low self-esteem, a fear of others, a guilt and shame that they seek to hide from other people - but always the feelings of "not being good enough" or "feeling dirty" remain.

The victim of abuse might seek relief in alcohol, drugs, food, work, and if they are introduced to a dysfunctional religion at a vulnerable moment in their lives, it is easy to understand how they could become obsessive and compulsive in using religion to "escape" from their pain.

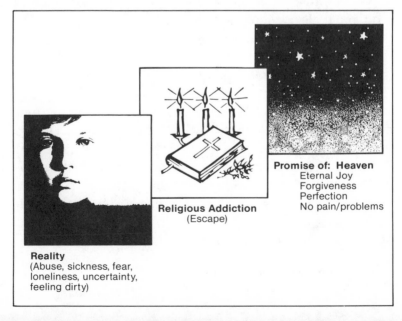

Promise of: **Heaven**
Eternal Joy
Forgiveness
Perfection
No pain/problems

Religious Addiction
(Escape)

Reality
(Abuse, sickness, fear,
loneliness, uncertainty,
feeling dirty)

BREAKING THE CHAINS

To a child who had been physically, sexually, or emotionally abused, life could easily appear nasty, cruel, frightening, and painful: Then somebody suggests

> a gentle Jesus, meek and mild,

> a God "out there" who would take away all the problems,

> the Holy Spirit entering your body and taking away all the pain,

> becoming a member of the purified with Heaven as your reward,

> the need to avoid the physical, sexual, and the material world.

After years of abuse, such suggestions would seem very attractive! A large percentage of religious addicts who have discussed their religious addiction revealed that they had grown up in abusive homes.

(c) *Children from religiously addicted families*:

All the research indicates that children from dysfunctional homes are affected by that dysfunction. Unless they face it, confront it, talk about it, they will take that "baggage" into adulthood. Research concerning alcoholism indicates that children born into an alcoholic home are at "high risk" of themselves becoming alcoholic; indeed, many adult children of alcoholics do not drink alcohol because of their fear of becoming alcoholic. However, whether they drink or abstain, they still have been affected by their environment.

A large number of children from parents who have a religious addiction also will grow up to be religious addicts or suffer from a dysfunctional behavior pattern (abuse) concerning religion. The dysfunction might reveal itself as rejecting any consideration of a religious message, or not seeing any merit in a religious view of the world, because of the pain and anger caused by their parents' religious addiction and abuse. This is similar to the behavior of the anorexics who say they do not abuse food because they do not eat! However, the behavioral disorder still concerns food, the focus is food, and the dysfunction is seen in the "control" they assert by not eating. Similarly, the child of a religious addict who "throws the baby out (i.e. concept of a creative God) with the bath water (dysfunctional religion)" is still affected.

However, a large number of these children grow up adopting the same religious style as their religiously addicted parents.

They condemn Jews (non-Christians) because they do not accept Jesus.

They reject other Christians who do not accept their interpretation of scriptures or holy writings - saying that they will not be "saved."

They have a puritanical view of sex.

They view life in black or white terms - an ongoing battle between God and Satan. Education, medicine and science must teach in accordance with their understanding of scripture.

They isolate from "the worldly" - which might include dancing, theater, drinking or relationships with the opposite sex.

They become "hooked" on a particular church, preacher, guru, or religious approach - discounting the concept of a multi-religious society.

They will not allow any doubts, questions, criticisms or alternatives to their religious approach.

They suffer severe bouts of depression, anxiety, guilt and shame should they break any of the strict religious rules.

Naturally, this condition will continue into the next generation unless there is an intervention, a crisis, or a "moment of sanity."

Many children from religiously addicted families marry religious addicts. Should we not be surprised? The children growing up in a religiously addicted household were isolated from secular society and only encouraged to mix with children who shared the same beliefs or went to the same church, synagogue or mosque. Naturally, significant relationships would be formed in these groups. The possibility of breaking away from this sick religious system is compounded by these friendships that reinforce the dysfunction; often the feelings of being trapped continue into marriage.

Claudia Black, in her book, *It Will Never Happen To Me*, quotes Cindy (34), saying:

As I was growing up, I remember really wanting only one thing - to be able to do it differently than I saw it being done around me, so, when, two days before my 23rd birthday, my husband was put in jail for a felony DUI, I looked into the passive eyes of my child whom I had just thrown across the room, and felt my world and my sanity crumble. I was doing it just the same way they had done. Two days later, I was in therapy with a psychologist who introduced me to Al-Anon and within a year I began to learn to do it differently. For the first time in my life, I began to see I had a choice. What a miraculous concept. I was building myself into a whole person even though my husband's alcoholism progressed rapidly for the next six years.

My husband has now had five years of sobriety. We learned this is a family illness and there can be family recovery if at least one family member tries to find alternatives. I am finally doing it differently, and for me, it is a better way. At last, finally, I had a choice.[6]

The tragedy is that few religious addicts realize or have the strength and support to act as Cindy. The information available to children growing up surrounded by religious abuse is almost nonexistent compared to those suffering from alcohol and drug abuse.

(d) *The Old:*

I suppose everybody, at some time, has a fear of dying. Our society finds many ways of avoiding the reality of death, which include:

Using expressions like "he has passed on" or "crossed over" or "gone to eternal rest."

Painting the faces of the dead in their coffins so

that they look healthier than when they were alive.

Avoiding the reality of age by face lifts, wrinkle creams, and rejuvenation injections.

Placing an over-emphasis on youth in:

fashion	movies
music	theatre
magazines	literature
education	sports.

Putting the old and elderly in "convalescent homes" or hospitals so that family members are spared the reality of the aging process.

This denial on the part of society not only keeps the reality of death from the young and middle-aged, but places an unhealthy anxiety in those who are old and close to death. An overpowering fear becomes the prevailing characteristic of the aged.

Also, the aged were brought up, as children, with a more emphatic religious structure. They attended Sunday school, read the Bible, had prayer said at school assembly, went to church on Sundays, avoided meat on Fridays and believed (because of a lack of travel, TV, racial and cultural interchange) that their "religious way" was the only way to behave. People in their sixties and over, for the most part, kept the faith of their families and were not encouraged to doubt, question or criticize.

Some "drifted" from the church in their middle years and, in old age, suffered feelings of guilt, remorse, and fear - because as children they were warned by their religious teachers about the dire consequences, if they "left the faith."

>They became anxious about dying and going to hell;

>They feared not being with family members in heaven;

>They had guilt about their misspent youth;

>And they knew they had little time to make it up!

These same crippled, lonely, frightened and infirmed old people were living in apartments, convalescent homes, hospitals, or with families across the nation and their one main comfort was television - particularly religious television. And it is here that the TV evangelists cast their spells. They preached forgiveness, healing, eternal life, a relationship with Jesus, reunion with dead family members, peace and comfort in death, escape from the fires and torments of hell - all these messages were attractively presented, incorporating music and old-fashioned hymns that rekindle past memories and they worked their charm. The aged were encouraged to sing praise at home, touch the hand of the evangelist by pressing their hand upon the TV screen, pray for forgiveness and absolution...*and of course, send in their donations!*

Naturally, such a group would be extremely susceptible to religious addiction or abuse. They were being promised, at the end of their lives, the ultimate "high" - eternal happiness and joy with God. All they needed to do was *believe*. Believe and pay!

Many of the aged seek freedom from physical pain by an abuse of prescription drugs. Why, then, should we be surprised that many were abused and became addicted around religion? The powerful and comforting message that all religions bring can easily be manipulated into an abusive and addictive "mind-set" by the unhealthy purveyors of religious addiction.

Even though the (monetary) gift met the divinely ordained total that (the Rev. Oral) Roberts had announced, he continued his fast in the Prayer Tower and asked his flock for more cash. Roberts' performance caused (Jimmy) Swaggart to lament, "The gospel of Jesus Christ has never sunk to such a level."[7]

(e) *The Sick:*

As with the old, the sick are particularly vulnerable. All the religions of the world contain stories of healings, miracles that reveal the power of God in His universe. It is, therefore, understandable that many people are attracted to religion because of the possibilities of miraculous healings - especially if doctors seemed unable to cure or heal the disease.

However, many of the spiritual leaders in all the major religions have also seen the dangers and superficiality of such an attraction. True religion seeks to heal the inner "spirit" of man and not just the outer surface.

True discipleship is often exemplified not so much in removing suffering but rather in learning how to live with it and use it for the glory of God.

In my book, *Spirituality and Recovery*, I seek to explain the difference between miracle and magic.

Many religious people, in ignorance, pray for magic. Want magic, ask for magic. It reminds me of Jesus' desert temptations at the beginning of His ministry.

"Jesus returned from the Jordan full of the Holy Spirit, and was led by the Spirit into the desert, where he was tempted by the Devil for forty days. In all that time, he ate nothing, so that he was hungry when it was over.

"The Devil said to him, 'If you are God's Son, order this stone to turn into bread.'

"But Jesus answered, 'The scripture says man cannot live on bread alone.'

"Then the Devil took him up and showed him in a second all the kingdoms of the world. 'I will give you all this power and all this wealth,' the Devil told him. 'It has all been handed over to me, and I can give it to anyone I choose. All this will be yours, then, if you worship me.'

"Jesus answered, 'The scripture says, "Worship the Lord your God and serve only him!"'

"Then the Devil took him to Jerusalem, and set him on the highest point of the Temple, and said to him, 'If you are God's Son, throw yourself down from here. For the scripture says, "God will order his angels to take good care of you." It also says, "They will hold you up with their hands so that not even your feet will be hurt on the stones."'

"But Jesus answered, 'Do not put the Lord your God to the test.'

"When the Devil finished tempting Jesus in every way, he left him for a while."

What kind of Messiah was He going to be? Would He feed the poor by changing stones into bread? No!

Would He do a deal with the Devil to gain political power over all the Kingdoms? No!

Would He offer circus spectacles from Temple roofs? No!
Jesus would offer no such mighty signs. No theatricals.
No magic. So many religious people forget this message and seek the supernatural fix. They want God to work the trick in their lives.
Take away the problems.
Remove the sickness or disease.
Stop the divorce.
Get Alice through college.
Keep George off the booze.
"God, will you work the magic?"
God is the universal drug of choice. Get high on religion. The Jesus trip. Say the prayer and the pain is gone. For a while it seems to work. But it does not last. It is not real.[8]

It is easy to understand why such a sick person would be attracted to a message that promised physical healing. A mother with a child suffering from leukemia would do anything to promote healing and out of a mixture of anxiety, fear, hope, and belief, would send money for a miracle. Such emotionally charged situations are obviously open to abuse. It is tragic that in the name of God, many fall victims to manipulation and religious fraud. All the more reason for those of us who preach the gospel to emphasize the inner miracle of self love (based upon God's love and acceptance of us all) rather than flamboyant healings, that have all the trappings of a circus.

This is not to suggest that physical healings and "miracles" beyond man's understanding do not take place - but they cannot be predicted by the whim of any preacher or mullah! Here, is a prayer that strikes the necessary balance:

O heavenly Father, we pray for those suffering from diseases for which at present there is no cure. Give them the victory of trust and hope, that they may never lose their faith in thy loving purpose. Grant thy wisdom to all who are working to discover the secrets of disease, and the faith that through thee all things are possible. Amen. (George Appleton)[9]

In requesting God's Love we already are being healed, and suffering might be part of that healing process.

(f) *The Young:*

Many young people, especially adolescents, are looking for "something definite" in a world (and body) that is constantly changing. The attraction to the "black and white," what is absolutely "right" and also what is absolutely "wrong," brings with it a certain power and authority.

Young people often seek to identify in fashion, music, gangs, and also religion. There is something romantically appealing in following an extreme set of religious demands, almost like an endurance test, that sets a person apart from the rest. The attraction of belonging to God's "chosen," a remnant that will shine in the darkness of this world, creating a "difference" that will get you noticed, is in itself appealing to many young people. The Ayatullah Khomeini is fanatically supported by the young people of Iran. Films of those involved in the various cults across the world reveal a high percentage of young people who are looking for "the way" - remember the Beatles and Maharesh Yoga! Many of the more "extreme" Christian denominations attract the young, often separating them from family and friends, making excessive demands that include acts of severe fasting and flagellation; wearing special robes and medallions, and following a "dress code."

We must not forget the element of "escape" that religious addiction can have for the young. We have seen this dramatically emphasized with the epidemic use of drugs and the creation of a youth "drug culture." They escape from the pain and loneliness of adolescence by an abusive and compulsive use of alcohol, drugs, cigarettes, excessive physical exercise, and an attachment to people (peer pressure). I would also like to add the excessive aspects of religion. David Hancock, in his pamphlet, "Points for Parents," states:

In dealing with problems of drug abuse and chemical dependency, we are basically dealing with problems of philosophy of life, of faith, of theology even. A common saying among recovered alcoholics is, "I was seeking God in a bottle." Some drugs can produce "welcome effects," can make you feel good. Let's be honest about it; they can.

But to look to alcohol and other drugs for the understanding of life, for the means of coping with its problems; to search for insight, for creativity, for the ability to love; to search for feelings of worthwhileness and for the attainment of one's full potential - to search for these through drugs and alcohol is nothing more than witchdoctoring and belief in magic - childishly unrealistic. There are no easy shortcuts to constructive, responsible, meaningful living. Booze and drugs may offer temporary escape, but they cannot really equip one better to deal responsibility with reality.[10]

Teenagers are necessarily not very sophisticated about life. They have a limited number of experiences in which to make judgments and so many young people will take "as gospel" what the preacher, priest or mullah says concerning what God wants. This naive appreciation of the variety of choice can lead to brainwashing, mind-control, and, of course, religious abuse.

FOOTNOTES

1. Davies, W. H. "POEM"
2. Turner, Tina, and Kurt Loder, *I, Tina*. (New York, William Morrow and Company, Inc., 1986) p. 167-8.
3. Ibid, p. 157.
4. King, Norman, *Everybody Loves Oprah!* (New York, William Morrow and Company, Inc., 1987) p. 45.
5. Ibid, p. 46.
6. Black, MSW, Claudia, *It Will Never Happen To Me*. (Denver, MAC, 1982) p. 150-1.
7. Ostling, Richard N., "TV's Unholy Row." *Time,* Vol. 130 (April 6, 1987) p. 67.
8. Booth, Fr. Leo, *Spirituality and Recovery - Walking on Water*. (Pompano Beach, Fla., Health Communications, 1985) p. 20-22.
9. Mollings, Fr. Michael, and Etta Gullick, *The One Who Listens*. (London, Mayhew-McCrimmond, Ltd., 1971). p. 111.
10. Hancock, David C., *Points For Parents Perplexed About Drugs*, (Minneapolis, Hazelden, 1975) p. 8.

Chapter 6

PERSONAL STORIES

The following stories give a comprehensive view of the types of people who become religious addicts or have been religiously abused; you will see that they are "all types and conditions of men." These stories have been compiled from letters, from conversations, telephone calls and personal "memories" recorded in my travels. Only the names have been changed to respect anonymity and confidentiality.

MARY'S STORY

Mary can never remember a time when she was not aware of religion in her life. Her first words spoken as a child were "Jesus" and "God" - not "mommy" and "daddy." Prayer, the Bible, Heaven - and the fear of Hell - made up most of her childhood experiences. Religion was always in her life.

She grew up in Akron, Ohio. Her mother and father were extreme fundamentalists, belonging to a church that was simply known as "the Church of God." And that explains exactly how they saw themselves. They were "the" church of God. From being a child she was told that her church was the only church, the faithful, the remnant, the people of Jehovah.

She was not permitted to make close friends with children who belonged to other Christian denominations. Jews, Roman Catholics (described as a cult by her preacher) and the "other" religions were considered heathen. Religion told her what she could not do: it was a "don't religion." Don't dance. Don't play on Sundays. Don't go to the movie house. Don't listen to the Beatles. Don't wear "sinful" clothes. Don't smoke. Don't drink. Don't curse. Don't complain. Don't answer back. Don't question. Don't. . . . The "don'ts" seemed endless.

She was expected to pray before every meal. Pray before she went to bed. Her mother and father prayed "extemporarily"; they were led by "the spirit," often speaking "in tongues" that she could never understand. Mary accepted that God was not to be understood. . . only obeyed. As she grew older she was expected to pray in the same manner. The sins that she had committed or imagined in the day were to be said aloud in her prayers; and she was expected to confess her sins before her parents.

Mary was an only child. As a child she remembered being very lonely. She would look out through the window and see the other children playing - but she was not allowed to play with them. She was made to feel "different." Evil seemed to include everything that everybody else did.

She remembered thinking that God's children were not supposed to have fun. Rarely was there laughter in her home. Life was strict, rigid and serious. She would kiss her mother and father on the cheek before going to sleep; never was she allowed to hug her parents. They never hugged her. She can never remember seeing her mother and father being affectionate toward each other.

Once, at about thirteen, she asked her parents where babies "were made." They told her to talk with the preacher. She remembered feeling that her parents were uncomfortable by the question, embarrassed. Never was sex discussed in her home. And yet the most embarrassing incident in her life occurred because of sex; it was her menstrual period. She was never told to expect a period. When she first started to bleed she honestly thought she had cut herself. For a long time she remembered searching for the cut! She was afraid to tell her mother, but in the end she had to; in her words "the bleeding got worse." Her mother gave her something to use. She did not explain or prepare Mary for what was happening, she simply said, "Put this over the bleeding." Again, the embarrassment.

The only thing that Mary was allowed to do, encouraged to do, expected to do, was eat. From her earliest days she remembered being fat. The only pleasurable thing in her life was eating; and it was okay! Food was allowed. She was expected to clean her plate. She could not have dessert until she had finished her "veggies." Often she would gag on the fatty meat, but when she tried to leave food, she was told, "Think of the starving children." Today she still finds it hard to leave food on her plate; she agonizes over "wasting food."

I met Mary in an eating disorder unit. She was twenty-six years old, about five-foot six inches and weighed 250 pounds. She was single and still lived with her mother. Her father had died when she was twenty. She looked frightened, lonely and very unhappy. She dressed like an old woman. She understood God to be a judge. She was afraid of Him. Mary was afraid of everyone.

I gave a lecture about "spirituality and recovery from

addiction" - referring to anger, isolation, and fear. Interestingly, Mary did not connect these feelings with her eating disorder, but she did connect them with her religion!

She told me that she was angry at her life; angry at her parents; angry about what she had missed. Much of what she had been told in her religion she no longer believed - but all her life she had *acted* as though she did believe; she never wanted to upset her parents. Mary said that all through her teenage years she hated going to church. Apparently it was a small church, less than 100 members. For most of her life she had been the youngest member! She was angry at her "people pleasing."

She hated the isolation that had made her feel different. Because she did not play or socialize with other children, she did not know how to talk with them at school. She hid behind books. She became an "A" student. But she was always lonely. She had no friends her own age; she talked "adult talk." She cleaned, ironed, washed, knitted and read the Bible. But there was always the food!

She said that she always loved her father, but was afraid of him. It went back to her being punished by him. He never played with her. Once, when she was about eight, she was caught skipping with a rope on Sunday - her father made her kneel on the skipping rope for an hour holding the Bible straight out in front of her. She has never forgotten that incident or the punishment. Mary spent the rest of her life trying to please her father.

And the feelings of anger, frustration, abandonment,

guilt, shame and fear were stuffed behind the food.

After her father died, she continued to go to church for about a year and then stopped. Her mother continued. Mary said she always felt uncomfortable around her mother. They were never really close. Mother continued to pray before eating, while Mary remained silent - waiting to eat!

Today, Mary talks about how her religion had "cut her off" from the real world. She was taught to hate people who did not think, act or believe as her family. And although deep down she never believed this, she kept her thoughts to herself - buried behind food. She remembered seeing beautiful children in Asia and thinking, How can these children be sent to Hell?

Mary is beginning to accept that her father was not a "bad" man, but a religious addict. His parents (Mary's grandparents) had believed the same strict faith and had passed it on; Mary's father was a child of a religious addict!

Mary's father was obsessed with his evangelical religion. He was at church every day, three times on Sunday. Religion, worship, meetings, Bible study, services of witness took priority over everything else in his life; he even missed Mary's high school graduation because he was engaged in a Christian convention! And yet he never appeared happy. It was not a happy or loving family.

When Mary heard lectures about addiction to food and alcohol, she recognized the same symptoms in her father's relationship with religion. Today she understands that her mother was religiously abused by her father's scriptural understanding of women; she was viewed as man's "help-mate." Mother was expected to obey, like Mary.

Today, Mary is working her O.A. (Overeaters Anonymous) program and going to A.C.O.A. (Adult Children of Alcoholics) meetings to learn about assertion and self-esteem; Mary is beginning to love herself. In her last letter, she said that she is discovering a God that she can understand - and He (She) is a friend!

CHARLES' STORY

I met Charles, who was black and lived in Chicago, after appearing on the Oprah Winfrey Show. We had been discussing religious addiction and I had suggested that some adult children escape into religion after growing up in an alcoholic home. At that point the light had gone on for Charles.

Charles had not grown up in a religious home. He was the youngest child of alcoholic parents. Throughout his childhood he experienced arguments, fights and beatings. He had two older brothers and often on weekends they would huddle together at night for comfort and protection - because they knew that their parents would be coming home drunk. Sometimes Dad did not come upstairs and disturb them. But often he did.

Dad would then pull them out of bed and start to beat on them. His reasons were incoherent. Charles remembered Mother standing at the bedroom door, holding a drink and smoking a cigarette! His older brothers were usually singled out for a heavy beating, and Charles was usually slapped across the face. But he felt the pain of his brothers. He said, "I remember chewing the sheets to stop myself from crying as I watched my brothers being beaten against the wall. Dad would use his fists, and the noise and screams were terrifying. My brothers, when they were younger, never fought back. But, at fourteen and fifteen, they began to defend themselves. They had had enough. But then it would get worse. Dad would beat them more!"

From his earliest days, Charles remembered embarrassment, fear, pain - and the thought of "escape." He often thought about suicide. As a teenager, he felt that life was "the pits." Adults were not to be trusted. Love was for other kids.

Then a friend took him to a mission chapel. He was about fifteen. He heard the preacher talk about the love of Jesus. He immediately liked the message. It was what he had longed to hear;

God loved him.

    Jesus loved him.

        Peace was within his grasp.

Charles told me that the hymns made him cry - but it was a "good cry." Singing about the love of Jesus, the faith of the saints, the coming of the Holy Spirit. He did not know if the tears were for Jesus or himself - perhaps both. At sixteen, after a sermon about witness, he gave himself to the Lord!

From that moment, he was hooked. He went to other chapels, churches, crusades, baptisms, Bible-study groups. He traveled to hear the "big" preachers and watched the T.V. evangelists. He especially liked the

"Old Time Gospel Hour" with Jerry Falwell. The old-style service reminded him of his conversion. He could never get enough of it. He not only considered himself as a disciple of Christ, but he believed he had a mission. He wanted to create a better world, a better society, more loving families - but it must be based upon Jesus. He read the Bible, learned appropriate texts and became convinced that Jesus was "the way, the truth and the life." The Bible was the absolute, literal "Word of God." Only fundamentalist Christianity was "the Truth."

Charles soon found himself at odds with others - especially his two brothers. At twenty-four, Charles was the only member of his family not drinking and doing drugs. His eldest brother was in jail. The next brother was married and had developed the lifestyle of his father - indeed, they all met and drank together. And always they ended up fighting!

But Charles took "the message" to others. He became active in a local fundamentalist church in south-side Chicago, reading and occassionally leading testimonies. His memory for Bible quotations was amazing, although he had no formal study in theology. But he could talk...and talk...and talk.

It became clear to Charles that happiness and joy could only be found in Jesus, and in the literal understanding of the "good news." For employment, he worked at a local radio station that employed some Roman Catholics and Jews. His mission began! He explained the Pope as the anti-Christ and told the Jews that as long as they rejected Jesus, they were outside salvation. Within six weeks, he had lost his job.

During this time he had met a girl (Anne) at the church and they had decided to get married. She was religious, a Christian, but did not read her Bible every day, pray before every meal, or "get high" planning the next Christian mission or crusade. She wanted her church, but she also wanted a family life; she wanted life.

Over the years, arguments developed - and they were all about religion. Charles decided Anne's faith was "lukewarm." He felt she put family before Christ. In a moment of anger she said, "Yes, I do! Being a Christian involves family life. I love you and I want an ordinary family life together. In loving family, we show our love to Jesus. But your demanding, rigorous faith is making it impossible." And then she said it: "Religion is like a drug to you!"

Charles specifically remembered Anne saying, "Religion is like a drug to you!" And that was the last straw for Charles. In a year they were divorced; they had had no children.

From this point in his life, things were either "up" or "down." For Charles, his narrow and rigid faith often created conflicts with the employers; often being away on a crusade, he did not get back for work on Monday. Also, he preached at the lifestyle of his fellow workers - resulting in termination. And he became depressed.

Charles also suffered from guilt. He never felt good enough for Jesus. He was always trying to do more, say more, give more, be more effective, convert more people, tithe more - be perfect. When he failed, he would emotionally beat himself up. Along with the depression came periods when he felt beseiged by "impure thoughts.'' The result was guilt and shame.

It was about this time that he watched the Oprah Winfrey Show and began to look at his behavior in the context of his childhood. He heard that many children of alcoholics became compulsive, obsessive and perfectionistic. Before watching the show, he had always thought that his childhood had made him difficult to live with. He had blamed his recent bouts of ''depression'' on his childhood and the state of the world. But after hearing about the symptoms of religious addiction, he began for the first time in his life to connect his pain and problems with his ''strict'' religion. He was open to the possibility that he had become obsessive about his faith - but he thought that all good Christians had to be obsessive about Jesus! And he also accepted that he had real problems and emotional pain, especially in the area of relationships. Only the church was in his life - and he had few Christian friends. He slowly began to accept that his extreme religious practices had not only created the divorce from Anne, but had placed a wedge between himself and most people. Charles was as isolated as any alcoholic he had ever met!

After a series of conversations, Charles was willing to consider that God might be involved with other Christian denominations - even Roman Catholicism! But more than this, Charles was able to connect his ''escape'' into an authoritarian religion with the abuse in his childhood. For years he had said that his brothers took drugs to escape their pain. Wasn't he doing the same with religion?

In our last conversation, he told me that he would attend some Fundamentalist Anonymous meetings, adding, ''I'm not promising anything!''

ALICE'S STORY

At the end of group meetings in the hospital, Alice would never hug me. She would never hug any man. She was afraid of men.

Monday morning I would conduct a "Spirituality group" for patients and it was here that I met Alice. She was an alcoholic. She was a Roman Catholic. But she intrigued me because she was a Roman Catholic who used the name of "Jesus" often, using the name "Jesus" more than "Our Lord" or "church" - she sounded more evangelical than Catholic!

She would say: "I love Jesus."
"I have given my life to Jesus."
"I am the bride of Jesus."

But her relationship with Jesus was not helping her reach out to other people and I felt that her faith had become an escape. But from whom was she escaping? What was she unwilling to face in her life? Why this obsessive relationship with Jesus that excluded people?

These questions were to be answered when Alice did her "first step" in group. The first step of A.A. states, "We admitted we were powerless over alcohol and that our lives had become unmanageable." Alice spoke about her childhood. Her father was an alcoholic, a very violent alcoholic. The family lived in fear of father's drunken behavior. Alice became the "lost child" in the family. She withdrew from the family with her pain.

In later life, after leaving home, she found alcohol. She immediately became addicted. Alice became a solitary drinker. She drank to escape the pain and loneliness that constituted her life. She drank to forget her childhood. But alcohol only brought more pain.

BREAKING THE CHAINS

After Alice's "first step," Janet, a girl in the group, began to share; she could identify with Alice's fear of her father. But Janet's fear not only concerned her father's drinking; for years, as a child, she had been sexually abused. Always it started the same way; he would come home from the bar in the afternoon and ask her to sit on his lap. Always the same games; always the same result. And her mother always seemed to disappear!

As Janet shared her pain, Alice began to sob. Her sobbing became uncontrollable; the pain that had been buried "cried" out. Among the sobs came the cry, "Why? Oh why? Why did this have to happen? I hate men! I hate sex! Sex is filthy!"

Then it all began to make sense. Alice had sought to escape from her pain by developing a relationship with a "safe" man. Indeed the safest man in the world: Jesus. She could love Him. He could love her and there would be no pain. Jesus was about "pure love." She remembered the emphasis on being pure from her education by the nuns. Alice would push everyone aside to "keep pure."

Alice's sexual abuse, coupled with her religious education from the nuns and others, had made her believe that sex was dirty. She feared men because of her past experience with her father. Girls at school had reinforced this fear by saying, "Boys only want one thing...sex!" Alice withdrew into her private world with Jesus!

Alice had created her own religious abuse by using Jesus in the same way that she had used alcohol: to escape. She judged, condemned, isolated, and feared "people" (especially men). The precious gift of spirituality, developing a loving and healing relationship with herself and others, was being lost to her. Nobody could get close. Friends could not love her because she would not allow herself to be known - and her unhealthy relationship with Jesus was keeping her sick. The combination of alcohol and Jesus was killing Alice!

The group discussed the various covers or masks they had used to avoid being known - how they had manipulated people, friendships, family, jobs, the Bible, religion, and, yes, even God. At first Alice protested, but over the weeks, she began to see and "own" her manipulation of Jesus. The group worked on her letting go of the "pure Jesus" in order to experience the "man Jesus" - who is alive in our love of ourselves and others. Some in the group referred to texts like, "Love God and your neighbor as yourself," encouraging Alice to begin taking risks in order to love herself and others, including men.

Alice has not taken a drink in two years. Sometimes I see her at hospital meetings. Always she gives me a big hug!

DEBORAH'S STORY

Deborah had been brought up in an Episcopal family where religion was practiced without being extreme. The family went to church three times a year (Christmas, Easter and New Year's service) - nothing religiously compulsive about this family!

At the age of twenty-four, Deborah became pregnant and was not sure who the father was; she chose to have the child and be a single parent. Her family was supportive and Deborah told me that during this time she was not experiencing any particular guilt; just inconvenience. She had other friends who had babies out of wedlock - not unusual in Los Angeles.

The little boy was born and seemed perfectly healthy at seven pounds, four ounces. He was baptized Mark, after his grandfather. Deborah was so glad that she had kept the child. Motherhood seemed to suit her. She played, laughed, and talked with Mark all through the day - these were her happiest days.

When he was in his fifth year, Mark started to get "sickly." First it would start with a cold, then nausea, followed by a temperature - and he began to look pale. Then Mark complained about feeling tired - some days he just wanted to sleep. The doctor suggested Deborah take Mark for tests at the Children's Hospital in Long Beach and a specialist pediatrician ran several tests. Deborah will never forget the day she heard the news. Mark was outside with Grandma, playing with his "Rambo toy" and the doctor simply said, "Your son has leukemia. I shall run further tests; at the moment things do not look good."

She remembered asking, "Is he going to die?" She was shocked at her asking such a question.

"Things do not look good. But we'll run further tests."

Deborah looked through the glass door and thought: How can a child, playing with a toy, die? It must be a terrible mistake!

So a series of tests began, followed by more tests, followed by even more tests and Mark stayed in the hospital. The news was never optimistic.

Deborah kept asking, "Why?" Could she have done

anything to have stopped this from happening?

Then a neighbor, who had heard the news, asked if she had prayed. Of course she had prayed, was Deborah's reply.

"No" - replied the woman - had she prayed in faith?

At first Deborah was angry, but she then began to think: "Is this my fault?"

Was God punishing her for sex outside of marriage? Was this a test of faith?

Then Deborah started to watch religious TV. She prayed every day. She started going to church with her neighbor. It was about this time that she started to "get hooked."

She heard:

"Jesus could move mountains."

"Jesus heals if you believe."

"If you put your faith before everything, tithing and showing tangible 'signs' of your belief in Jesus, your prayers will be answered."

At this point, Deborah began making substantial payments to various TV ministries.

The doctors said they could do nothing; she felt Mark's life depended on her faith!

Some days Mark perked up, and had the energy to play with the Rambo toy. Was this a "sign" that he was healed? Mark was getting better - Deborah sent more money!

Deborah prayed many times a day. She sent money nearly every week. When Mark relapsed, Deborah decided to send her life savings.

On TV she had heard:

"How much faith do you really have in Jesus?"

"Do you put other things before your faith?"

"Can you take your wealth with you?"

"Jesus healed the lepers. Jesus healed the paralyzed. Jesus healed the blind. Why should you doubt the healing power of Jesus?"

"Put your hand on the TV screen and pray with me. Cast away every doubt. Believe."

"Can you feel the Holy Spirit entering into you? Name the person you want the Holy Spirit to heal. Name the child."

Deborah cried, shouted, screamed, "Mark! Mark! Oh, please God - Mark!"

Many years after Mark had died, Deborah spoke to me because she was still angry - but she was angry at herself. Mark had died two weeks before his eighth birthday and Deborah had to borrow money from her parents for the funeral. She had given away everything. The more desperate Mark's health became, the more she felt the need to "prove" her faith.

And Deborah was angry at God. Angry at Jesus. Angry at Bible teaching. Angry at the TV preacher. But she was always angry at herself!

Our talk helped her understand about religious abuse. Deborah could identify with the feelings of a co-dependent wife who had wanted her alcoholic husband healthy at any price. Deborah recognized the symptoms:

denial	bargaining
manipulation	fear
loneliness	desperation
control	guilt
anger	rage
	"emotional death."

At the time of Mark's death, she wanted to sue the preacher. But suing the preacher would not bring Mark back. She has since watched the same TV preacher and she understands the "cunning, baffling and powerful" message: "If you do this, believe this and send money - something good will happen." Deborah had allowed her vulnerable feelings concerning Mark's leukemia to become the "stick" by which she was religiously abused. As with the co-dependent's relationship with the addict, she was loving too much - and creating abuse in her life.

Deborah was asking for help. At the time of writing, I could only suggest the co-dependency groups that meet in the Los Angeles area around the theme "Women Who Love Too Much."

BREAKING THE CHAINS

I have since watched many TV religious preachers and I can see how people get hooked, spellbound and obsessed/addicted to the "healing" message. True, suffering people will hear what they want to hear; however, I feel that a responsible evangelist should do everything to stop the possibility of "abuse" in the name of God! All ministers need to be accountable for the message that they attribute to God. Taking Biblical healing stories out of context is crude salesmanship - and worse, emotional blackmail!

PAUL'S STORY

Paul knew from the age of twelve that he was a homosexual. But he kept it hidden. As a child, he had attended the local neighborhood church in Marietta, Georgia, and he remembered hearing that being homosexual was the "worst" sin; the unspeakable sin. That being the case, how could he ever tell anybody? How could he tell his family?

Paul was not a "jock." He had had asthma as a child and, although he played sports, he was not very good at them - but he tried. He did not want to be considered a sissy. He learned how to act tough, walk "butch" and associate with the gang! But always he had homosexual feelings.

He shared with me an incident that was very difficult for him to talk about. When he was fifteen he was bicycling through a park and he stopped to use the restroom. He sensed he was not alone and as he stood at the stall a young man came and stood at the next stall.

Nothing was said, but he felt the excitement. He realized that the young man was masturbating and Paul immediately became erect. He was nervous and scared - and yet excited. He looked away, but it seemed as though he was being drawn into the activity. Soon he was showing himself to the young man. A noise outside the restroom scared the young man and he left. Throughout this encounter not a word was spoken!

Paul learned two things from this experience; (1) he was not alone, and (2) he liked what had happened.

Paul's family was friendly with the minister at church and one evening after dinner Paul made up a story that was loosely based upon the incident. He said that he had used the restroom in the park and saw two men looking at each other. He said he immediately left. What did it mean? Paul wanted to know what the family and minister really felt.

The minister became incensed and exclaimed, "These people are the lowest of the low. They are the scum of the earth. They defame the sacred image of God. They are an abomination. Their punishment will be the unquenchable fires of Hell!"

His parents said, "Don't go in that park again."

The incident ended with the minister saying he would write a letter to the police superintendent (who attended the Baptist church) and have the restroom placed under surveillance. Paul began to feel shame. That night he asked Jesus to remove his impure thoughts, his "dirty feelings" and forgive him.

All through high school and college Paul kept his sexual feelings to himself; but they never left. Then he went with some Christian friends to a crusade conducted by Rev. Jimmy Swaggart. Swaggart referred to the horrible sin of homosexuality that was seducing many young men in America and he prayed that the Holy Spirit would heal all those who renounced Satan and his evil practices and embrace the Lord.

Paul felt an upsurge of feelings, and with tears in his eyes went forward to embrace the Lord. He gave himself to the Lord in that service. From that crusade, religion became like a drug to him. He could not get enough prayer, crusades, fastings, missions, and personal witnessing. He became rigid, dogmatic, judgmental - basing all his personal behavior on scripture. He was particularly antagonistic and judgmental towards homosexuals. Today he admits, understandably when you consider his environment and history, that he was homophobic. He made statements like,

"All queers are going to Hell!"

"Homosexuals are child molesters and spread disease."

"Gay teachers should be removed from schools."

"Only when a homosexual repents of his sin and perversion can he be saved."

Paul became a reader and elder in the church. He married a girl who belonged to the Assembly of God - but they had no children.

He says that all the time he was saying these things, having girl friends, preparing for marriage - he still had, buried deep within himself, homosexual feelings. He rationalized it as his personal battle with Satan; Satan was trying to get him!

When I met Paul, it was after a suicide attempt. He could no longer live with himself; he could no longer live with his hypocrisy. The suicide attempt had followed his arrest for "lewd behavior" in a restroom. He told me he had never forgotten the excitement he had experienced as a youth in the park. Sexually, his marriage had been dead for years - if it was ever alive. His wife had been brought up to believe that sex was dirty and they had slept in separate beds for years. And his homosexuality had never left him.

Paul's story was reminiscent of another young man, Steve, who told his story to the U.S. News (October 1987):

His father (Free Will Baptist) insisted he see a psychiatrist. "Maybe he can change you," he said, "and make you normal." An aunt donated money to Oral Roberts, beseeching the television evangelist to pray for her nephew. "Steve could help," she said, "by getting up on Sunday, donning a suit and placing his hand on the TV set while Roberts preached."

ELIZABETH'S STORY

Elizabeth's daughter wrote to me from Kansas City. Her mother had given all her savings to a church because she wanted to go to Heaven! This is her story.

Elizabeth had lost her husband, Tom, two years earlier; neither of them had been active at church. They had been good God-fearing people, but they did not attend any church. They had raised three children and all of them had done well and gone off to start families of their own. The family met together once a year - but were not particularly close.

When Tom had died, Elizabeth remained at home, alone. She never talked about being lonely, but looking back on subsequent events, she was not only lonely but depressed and fearful as well. After Tom's death the rest of the family had picked up their lives where they had left off - and Elizabeth was left with a meaningless existence.

At this point Elizabeth turned to religion. When Tom was alive, they had never watched the religious channels, but now she turned to the television ministries for solace and comfort. She wanted to feel the "spirit" of Tom. She wanted to be reunited with him in Heaven. She was afraid of dying. She was experiencing a little guilt, especially when she heard on TV the hymns and prayers she would sing as a girl growing up in Kansas. Elizabeth felt guilty about not going to church (she had only attended Sunday school) and she had never been confirmed; she had never tithed or "given" to the church - and yet she had always tried to live a Christian life.

Being a senior citizen (Elizabeth was seventy-seven), fearful about "life after death," she was vulnerable to the dramatic statements that are commonplace in many television ministries.

"Give up everything and follow me."

"Unless you turn to Jesus and accept Him as your Lord and Savior, there will be no inheritance."

"Membership of the family of God in Heaven is earned by our earthly witness."

"Send your money - don't delay - Christ's ministry is dependent upon your response."

"Become a cheerful giver for the Lord."

The combination of guilt, fear and loneliness started Elizabeth sending checks in the mail for various TV ministries; she sent money she could not afford. None of the family was aware of these donations and over a period of six months, Elizabeth had sent all her savings. Incredible. Horrendous. At the age of seventy-seven, Elizabeth was destitute!

I'm sure no TV preacher would ever want to see an old lady destitute; however, the central core of many homilies, coupled with selected scriptural texts, concerns money - and this can lead to abuse. An addiction/abuse process can be created, especially if the reward is Heaven. Not only Heaven, but an ever-lasting relationship with loved ones who have gone before - spouses, parents, grandparents and friends. In this sense, religion is a most powerful agent - perhaps the most powerful agent in the world - and is open to abuse by the naive or unscrupulous. I believe that the senior citizens are the largest contributing group to the TV ministries.

One such lady who could be included in this category was Elizabeth.

ROBERT'S STORY

Theo and Martha waited to see me after I had presented a lecture on "Intervention - and the Religious Addict" at an addiction conference. I knew they had a serious problem; they looked anxious, agitated and very frightened. Martha spoke, "We're here to talk about our son. We want to arrange for an intervention."

They could identify with everything I had said about the symptoms of religious addiction. Their son, Robert, had a "religious problem" and it was affecting them.

Robert, at about the age of twenty-one, had gone to stay at an old Catholic monastery with a friend during his vacation from college. Theo and Martha were Greek Orthodox and attended church regularly - Robert had always gone with them when he was at home, but he was not especially religious. So his visit to the monastery was surprising, but not unusual. They thought he was catching up on academic studies.

Returning to college, he stopped off at home and said he had very much enjoyed the experience at the monastery; he had learned a great deal and would like to go back soon. His parents did not think any more about it. Then Robert, almost immediately, started writing letters and receiving letters from the abbot. Also, behavioral changes began to happen. Robert went to church every day; he stopped seeing his girlfriend; he began to talk about the church, the sacraments, and the saints. Some days he would not eat, saying he was fasting. When Martha began to complain about his diet, he said he was "under instructions from the old Catholic abbot."

When his next vacation came around, Robert informed his parents that he would be home for only a few days because he was returning to the monastery. His parents became angry and concerned - naturally feeling neglected. Theo and Martha tried to get Robert to reconsider, but Robert was adamant.

He returned home after his long stay at the monastery and Martha said he looked "awful." He had lost more than ten pounds and looked tired; seeming "distant." The remarks he made before returning to college were out of character:

"Jesus expects total dedication."

"Sometimes a Christian must choose between God and his family."

"The concepts of sacrifice and suffering are essential for spiritual growth."

His parents were afraid - and yet helpless. Martha's words, "Father Leo, I knew I was losing him. He was like Jekyl and Hyde. But how could I fight a church? I needed to know what they were saying to him."

Martha told me that she did something that she had never done before; she read some of the letters he had received from the abbott. Apparently Robert was "under instruction" in preparation for becoming a novice, before becoming a monk. Martha was shocked! The tone of the letter was authoritarian and rigid:

He must pray at least for 20 minutes, three times a day.

He must fast (no food or beverages) - only water - at least once a week.

If he had impure thoughts, he should thrash himself with a "purifying whip." He was also expected to wear a type of "hair shirt" garment under his clothes.

He must not be alone with a female - except for family.

He must avoid the "ungodly." (This seemed to include not only non-Christians, but also those who did not keep the "orthodox Catholic faith."

The rules and disciplines of "the order" must not be shared with anyone.

Going to movie houses or dancing was forbidden.

He needed to attend the Eucharist (Mass) on Sundays and all Feast Days.

Martha talked to Theo and they agreed not to mention anything to Robert until his next return from college. During telephone conversations, which were invariably initiated by Martha, Robert seemed cold and distant - often quoting scripture, condemning fellow students or talking about the teachings of the church. It was not unusual, nowadays, for Robert to ask Martha to pray with him on the telephone!

When Robert returned from college for Christmas, he again announced he would only be home for a few days because he intended to spend Christmas at the monastery. Theo and Martha confronted Robert about the letter and the instructions from the Abbot. Martha told Robert that she knew she had done wrong by opening his mail, but she was worried out of her mind and she felt that not only was she losing her son but that he was being controlled.

Robert became extremely angry and began to make incoherent statements. Theo and Martha remembered some of them:

> They (Theo and Martha) were coming between him and Jesus.
> They were not Christians, anyway, because they did not follow the teachings of the Church.
> He had decided to put "the Church" and God before his sinful and apathetic family.
> Prying into his letters only proved they were "in collusion with Satan."
> The world was coming to an end and only the "pure" would be saved.
> The lives of the saints and the Blessed Virgin Mary were the model for Christians - parents only had authority when they reflected such sanctity.
> Non-Catholics were damned.
> They should be "proud" of their devoted son.
> He was going to leave college and join the "novitiate" at the monastery - finishing his studies at the monastery.
> He would never sleep at home again.
> He would communicate with them only through letters; and when the Abbot allowed it they could visit him at the monastery, if they wished.

Martha and Theo were devastated. Then they became angry. But always they felt helpless.

BREAKING THE CHAINS

Robert left home and went into the monastery, giving up his last year at college! Theo and Martha have not seen their son since he left more than a year ago. Martha writes every month; Robert has written two letters!

Theo and Martha appeared like many parents I have seen affected by the drug habit of their children; addiction is a family disease. Religious addiction hurts the same way.

Because Robert is in a monastery and his parents are not allowed to visit him, it is impossible to arrange a meeting or discover the facts. Naturally, I am aware that the information I have been given might not be exactly true - Martha's co-dependency characteristics were quite apparent. But they did show me some letters that Robert had sent them since his early association with the monastery, plus odd scribblings on post-cards; not the writings of a healthy young man in his twenties!

I agreed to write a non-threatening letter to Robert, introducing myself as a friend of the family and hoping I might meet with him when time allowed, suggesting I might visit him at the monastery. To date, I have received no acknowledgement or reply.

RITA'S STORY

Rita wrote to me after a radio "call-in" where we were discussing religious addiction. She could identify with the symptoms and had been helped by Fundamentalists Anonymous - although she was also going to ACoA meetings.

Rita, from childhood, had been the achiever in the

family. In ACoA terms, she was the "family mascot." Both her parents were alcoholic and she blamed herself. She was an only child. She experienced no physical abuse, but she knows she was emotionally hurt; her parents were simply not there for her. She felt abandoned.

At school she became an "A" student and tried to gain her parents' love and attention by being a success. When I asked if she was religious, she said that she had been raised "Episcopal" - but had never really gone to church. Not an unusual practice among Episcopalians!

At nineteen, Rita had a traumatic shock; her parents were killed in an automobile accident. They had both been drinking! Now Rita was physically alone. She felt robbed, angry, isolated and afraid.

Rita was at college at the time of the accident and so many students invited her to meetings and socials on the campus; they knew it was not good for her to be alone. It was at one such meeting that she met Alan. He was not very attractive, but he expressed a sincere concern and asked, specifically, if she was a Christian. He invited her to attend some Bible study groups that were being held at the homes of different students, suggesting that she might get some questions answered. She agreed to go.

That was the beginning of her relationship with Alan. He did not belong to any particular denomination - although he was an extreme fundamentalist. He said that drinking was a sin and it did not "pay" - hence her parent's accident! He told Rita that she was a "child of God" and that Jesus loved her very much; this Rita wanted and needed to hear. Rita said she would strive to be a faithful disciple, basing her life on the teaching of Scripture.

Being a perfectionist, an overacheiver, the "mascot" of the family and an "A" student, Rita put everything into her religion. Together, Alan and Rita became known as the "converting duo." Every evening was spent attending Bible study, creating worship services, planning missions, answering questions, attending healing services, etc., etc. Rarely was Rita alone with Alan. But, naturally, she would never complain!

Within the year, they were married. Rita told me that everything before the marriage and after the marriage revolved around religion; the symptoms of religious addiction applied to them.

The major problem for Rita happened in the bedroom - or rather did not happen in the bedroom. Alan did not want to have sex! For the duration of their marriage, the performance in the bedroom was

> read a Bible story,

> say prayers; hold hands for the coming of the Holy Spirit,

> a kiss on the cheek,

> the lights out,

> sleep.

Rita tried to reach out to him - but he pushed her away. Alan said that sex was sinful because it aroused in people "base passions."

From that moment, Rita began to question, within herself, what was happening.

She also saw in her relationship some of the symptoms that she had recognized in her parents: the denial, the blaming, the no-talk rule, manipulation, running to scripture (bottle) to solve every problem, isolation and no "real" communication. Rita sensed what was happening; it was deja vu. Her self-esteem had been abysmal during her childhood - it was worse in this marriage. All Alan wanted to do was work, pray, read scripture, and eat large dinners, followed by ice cream. Alan gained weight - Rita lost weight.

Rita had become a "religious slave" in the household. Alan did not physically abuse her, but he mentally and emotionally made her feel inferior. He made her feel ashamed of her sexuality, ashamed of being a woman!

Alan believed that:

> Satan was championing the feminist movement and that the Christian place for a woman was in the home, at the stove.
>
> The Jews were to blame for most of the world's problems. They were leading all these liberal causes.
>
> Eve seduced Adam for sex. And sexuality would destroy the world - look at AIDS!

After hours of "pontificating," Alan would sit in front of religious television. Rita would cook, Alan would eat...then they would sleep. Rita could take it no more. For the past year she had "mouthed" a faith but did not believe it. She began to loath Alan. She saw his idleness in the home (excused by manipulating scripture) and she hated the hypocrisy. She knew that they were hiding from the real world, hiding from themselves - and she wanted out!

An opportunity came. Alan's employers were moving to Ohio. More money and less expense. Alan was delighted. God was repaying Alan's stewardship!

Rita refused to go; she wanted to stay in Los Angeles - she wanted out of the marriage. Alan was shocked. This was the only time he hit her. He said Rita's refusal was Satan talking. Rita said it was Rita talking for the first time. She was proud of herself.

After he left to go to Ohio, Rita went into therapy and she was recommended to Fundamentalists Anonymous. At F.A. meetings, Rita met many members who also attended ACoA meetings; she began to realize that she was not alone.

When I talked with Rita and heard her story (and recovery) I wondered how many millions of Ritas there were "out there." Hopefully, these stories will enable them to experience the recovery that comes from discovering the miracle within.

Oh, yes - Rita is still a Christian. She has returned to her Episcopal church and attends about once a month; not bad for an Episcopalian!

PART TWO:

THE SOLUTION

Chapter 7

INTERVENTION

The question is often asked, "How do you help somebody with a drinking problem who does not want help? Doesn't the alcoholic have to reach 'rock bottom' before he or she can receive help?" The answer to these questions is "No!" It is possible to assist a person into treatment; it is possible to encourage a family into treatment; creating a realistic awareness can and usually does precipitate change - intervention. Intervention is a harsh, sharp and unbending word. However, it is a word that creates a "loving moment," allowing healing and recovery to begin for a life, for a relationship, for a family.

Intervention is about "seeing";
    intervention is about reality;
        intervention is 'tough love' molded into action.

The craft of intervention has been used successfully in getting alcoholics, drug addicts, and people with obsessive and compulsive behaviors to face their lives, to really see the pain that is affecting them and their loved ones. The result is treatment, therapy, and a Twelve-Step support group. I believe this same technique needs to be applied to religious addiction.

Vernon Johnson, in his pioneer book on intervention, *I'll Quit Tomorrow*, explains:

It became clear to us that it was not only pointless but dangerous to wait until the alcoholic hit bottom. The inevitable crises could actually be employed to break through the alcoholic's defenses, an act of intervention that could stop the downward spiral towards death. We came to understand that crises could be used creatively to bring about intervention. Because, in fact, in all the lives we studied it was only through crises that intervention had occurred. This led to experimentation with useful methods of employing crisis at earlier stages of the disease.

Over the years, people have charged the Institute with inventing a system of treatment based on creating crises. And our response is that we do not invent crises, that it is not necessary to invent it. Every alcoholic is already surrounded by crises, no one of which is being used constructively. All we have to do is make those around the alcoholic knowledgeable enough so that they can start using the crises. This makes it possible for the alcoholic to move sooner, and to limit the very real damage that comes from living with a worsening situation. . . .

Several misconceptions about alcoholism cause people to be fearful to confront alcoholics. We are told that the alcoholism may be a cover for some more serious emotional disorder, and that alcoholics can be shattered if they are cornered. Another misconception is that the alcoholic is heedless and does not care what damage such behavior causes. This leads to the erroneous assumption that the alcoholic will be unresponsive to any offers for help. Because of wide mood swings, the alcoholic is a formidable person to confront, and is able skillfully to rationalize this behavior. . . . the alcoholic does not smash so easily, and there is an explanation for careless behavior. Actually, the alcoholic is loaded with self-hatred, which is repressed and unconscious, and often projected onto other people.[1]

This is also true for the religious addict. To quote the key to Vernon Johnson's technique again, "All we have to do is to make those around the alcoholic knowledgeable enough so that they can start using the crisis."

People need to understand that religious addiction -religious abuse - creates a behavioral dysfunction, a crisis. Not unlike that which affects the alcoholic and his family, the crisis is desirable (i.e., it can be used to get a person help or into treatment). The symptoms of religious addiction are not only internal, but external, producing physical problems, a nervous and rigid affect, a dis-comfort (dis-ease) in lifestyle.

The miracle of healing will only begin when we can connect these symptoms with the disease, religious addiction. For example:

When we are able to understand and discern that the ecstatic cries of the young Muslims in Iran - with their intemperate behavior, their lust for blood and revenge, their willingness to "die for the cause," their isolation from others and prejudice towards other Muslims, their hatred of Jews as "the heathen" - this behavior exemplifies the symptoms of religious addiction, or at least religious abuse, that is triggered by a compulsive craving (addiction) around a particular religious message.

We need to compare the "denial" of the religious addict, the unwillingness to accept criticism or discussion, having a literal understanding of scripture according to a particular and narrow interpretation, a black-and-white approach to right and wrong, an arrogant condemnation of anybody who thinks differently - with the "powerlessness" and "unmanageability" that is seen in the lives of many alcoholics and addicts and their suffering family and friends.

We need to connect the excessive financial contributions of the old lady in Florida with her religious addiction concerning a TV evangelist; to link her secrecy in making a religious TV ministry the sole beneficiary of her "earthly savings" - with her belief that to enter

Heaven she needs to give away everything, and follow Jesus. Only then will we begin to understand religious abuse and religious co-dependency.

When will we be able to understand that a mother's compulsive and obsessive religious behavior concerning healing services, prayer marathons, Bible study and "crusades of witness" are linked to her understanding that her sick child will only be healed by an extreme commitment to a church, chapel or "belief system"? Perhaps the medical profession had been unable to predict recovery for her child and the mother's religious behavior is rooted in the believed message that the child's life is dependent upon her discipleship and witness. Here is another aspect of religious abuse.

Religious addiction, like all the other compulsive and obsessive behaviors, affects "whole" persons and they take their sickness into every relationship. In this sense religious addiction is a disease that can be observed in many instances for those with eyes to see. However, as we have already seen, the enemy of recovery is denial, and denial takes many forms. It might be helpful at this time to record the numerous characteristics of denial that keep the religious addict and the family dysfunctional.

Aspects of denial for the religious addict:

Rationalizing	Minimizing
Justifying	Evading, dodging
Projecting	Defiance

Blaming, accusing	Attacking, aggression
Judging, moralizing	Withdrawing
Intellectualizing	Silence
Analyzing	Verbalizing, talking
Explaining	Shouting, intimidating
Theorizing	Threatening
Generalizing	Frowning
Quibbling, equivocating	Glaring
Debating, arguing	Staring
Sparring	Joking
Questioning, interrogating	Grinning, smiling, laughing
Switching	Projecting
Being smug, superior, or arrogant	Agreeing
	Complying[2]

These are exactly the same defenses used by the alcoholic and the addict!

How do you help a religious addict who does not want help? Must we wait until the old lady in Florida is penniless? The wife divorced from the crusading husband? The children angry and resentful, often developing a similar dysfunction around religion? Must the baby die because a minister or church objects to a blood transfusion? Do we have to wait until the religious addict has reached rock bottom?

Again, the answer is a resounding, "No!" If you wait too long, it could be too late, not only for the religious addict but also for family, friends and those affected by the religious addict. *Remember, the symptoms of religious addiction always involve religious abuse.* Family and friends also need education, understanding, treatment and ongoing support!

(A) *Education:*

It is absolutely essential that family and concerned friends be educated to the fact that religious addiction is a disease, a compulsive and obsessive behavioral lifestyle that centers around God, the Bible, a church, guru, TV evangelist or particular belief system. Religious addiction creates a dynamic of codependency where the sufferer believes that they are serving God, loving God. However,

> they miss God's love for them,

> they miss the power of divinity in their lives,

> the creative power of responsible choice and change is lost to them,

> they view themselves as helpless servants,

they remain victims of shame and guilt,

the miracle of variety and "difference" in God's world - especially concerning worship and discipleship - is incomprehensible.

At a pre-intervention meeting, the family members and friends should study and discuss the symptoms of religious addiction, and more importantly, apply the symptoms to cite actual instances that they have observed. The symptoms that I have listed describe the "broad picture" that reveals the disease.

(B) *Help:*

It is important that family members realize that help is available. As with other compulsive behaviors, the biggest obstacle to recovery is an overwhelming feeling of helplessness. The disease of religious addiction has flourished in ignorance and apathy. Man's innate creativity is missed by an abuse of God and religion and once we begin to talk about it, help is realized.

It has been my experience that after the initial meeting, when instances and painful incidents are related, the family experiences fear and feelings of "it will never work." It is at this time that the interventionist needs to be optimistic, pointing out that if the behavior is going to be changed, then something needs to be done; action must accompany words of concern.

Perhaps inviting a member of FA (Fundamentalists Anonymous) to this pre-intervention meeting would be helpful so that family members can meet a person recovering from religious addiction and experience the message of hope.

(C) *Understanding:*

At the pre-intervention meeting, time needs to be taken to explain that the religious addict is not a "bad" person, but a sick person. Their dysfunctional behavior has progressed because of the belief that they are doing what God expects or demands. This dysfunctional behavior has come from somewhere; in the case of the religious addict it has either come from family, a TV evangelist, a church teaching, etc., etc. Often, they have made themselves "victims" by exaggerating and twisting the original message.

Many religious addicts developed a "religious obsession" in order to avoid or escape from emotional pain in their lives - alcoholism, eating disorders, isolation, guilt, shame, sexual abuse, physical disfigurement, poverty, and financial insecurity. The religious obsession made them feel not only loved by God but also   special,

redeemed,
the chosen.

A sick self-esteem develops from an exaggerated understanding of "who they are" and then arrogance, prejudice, judgment and intolerance follow.

It is important to tell family members that no one grows up wanting to be an alcoholic. No one grows up wanting to be a child of an alcoholic. No one grows up wanting to have an eating disorder. A combination of hereditary factors, environment, unhealthy messages and a physical/psychological craving all converge to create "the disease factor"; this also is true for the religious addict.

(D) *Treatment:*

Just as we are able to successfully treat alcoholism and a variety of addictions, so I believe the same is true for religious addiction. Family members and friends need to have treatment as the goal of the intervention. We know that obsessive behavior is a process, not an event; it usually takes years of using and abusing drugs, listening to sick messages, nurturing the dysfunctional lifestyle before the thin line is crossed and we are into addiction. This is also true for religious addiction. People do not wake up one morning and become religious addicts; religious addiction usually follows years of religious abuse. The intervention, coupled with treatment, should be seen as the beginning of the *recovery process.* Once religious addiction is seen as a treatable disease, having symptoms similar to other addictions, then more and more treatment centers will be able to successfully treat the religious addict and family. This should be cause for great hope.

In Chapter 8, we will discuss a treatment modality for religious addiction.

(E) *Ongoing support:*

When I was leaving the hospital, after being treated for my own alcoholism, a counselor said, "Remember, Leo, treatment never ends!" And today I understand what he meant.

BREAKING THE CHAINS

The disease of addiction is never cured in the sense that it is removed; rather, we arrest the disease with a daily program of recovery. The Twelve-Step programs have proved essential to many addicts and co-dependents for not only making recovery possible, but also in discovering a spiritual process for living. This must also be true for the religious addict. Fundamentalists Anonymous has proved to be an important self-help program for many religious addicts. They come together for support, understanding and to share their pain with those who have been "through it" - those who understand. Fundamentalists Anonymous states:

(FA) is a national support organization for people who have been burned by the fundamentalist experience. (We use "fundamentalism" to include the charismatic/pentecostal movement.) We work with ex-fundamentalists as well as concerned parents, spouses, relatives and close friends of those caught up in fundamentalism.

FA is not an anti-Christian or atheistic group, but neither is it a front for any church or religion. We do not recruit satisfied fundamentalists: we only work with those who have decided to leave fundamentalism and need help.

People have a right to embrace fundamentalist beliefs. But we also have the right to leave fundamentalism and form our own support system. We are against any attempt to impose fundamentalist beliefs on the rest of society by coercion, intimidation, manipulation, or legislation. We also have the right and duty to make the public aware of our bad experiences in fundamentalism and to work with those who seek to escape this mindset, worldview and lifestyle. Our goals are twofold: 1) to help people make a successful transition from fundamentalism to a healthier lifestyle; and 2) to educate the public on how fundamentalism can be a serious mental health hazard to many.[3]

Because many interventionists and counselors will feel insecure, untrained and threatened by religious addiction, it would be helpful to have a member of Fundamentalists Anonymous come and talk to the treatment team and also support the family in preparation for the intervention on the religious addict. It might even be helpful if the *recovering* religious addict participates in the intervention itself - sharing some personal "moments."

I remember watching the Jewish author and Nobel prize winner Elie Weisel being interviewed on TV and he was asked the question, "Why do you keep talking about the holocaust? Why don't you let the world forget?" His response was clear and concise. "Once we forget, it will all come back." When I heard this interview, I immediately thought about recovery from addiction, especially religious addiction. We need to keep the memory alive; we need to remember what happened and how it happened: we need to keep alive the feelings of yesterday so that we can continue recovering for today. Every self-help group is a continuation of the intervention event. We create a program of rememberance.

(F) *Preparing for an intervention:*

After the above information has been given to the family and friends of the religious addict, it is important to prepare for the actual intervention.

I) The intervention should be seen more as a "loving encounter" rather than as a confrontation. Nothing is achieved by creating an abusive confrontation. The healing will only come for the religious addict when he/she understands and accepts that the messages at the intervention spring from love. For this reason it is important that the people who are involved in the intervention are loved, respected, admired, or play a meaningful part in the religious addict's life; mother, father, friend, significant other, children, aunt, uncle, colleague, employer, concerned clergy friend. There seems little point in having someone at the intervention whose presence would cause an adverse reaction for the religious addict. Creating unnecessary problems would only detract from the prime objective of the intervention.

II) Where should the intervention take place? The experience of many interventionists has been that the choice of people involved is more important than the place. However, taking the religious addict out of his own domain lessens his power and control over the situation, making him more vulnerable to hearing the message of concern. It is hard for the religious addict to throw everyone out of the house if he is not in his own home!

However, being overly dogmatic as to where to do the intervention only creates more problems; suffice to say that many a successful intervention has been done in the addict's home. The key to winning the game is in the players, not the field!

III) Because intervention is about sharing feelings and feelings are not readily identified by many people, let alone discussed, it would be good to study a feelings chart with the family. Family members and friends need to know what they are feeling. How living with a religious addict has affected them. The feelings chart will (*Continued on page 198*)

FEELINGS

AGGRESSIVE	AGONIZED	ANXIOUS	APOLOGETIC	ARROGANT	BASHFUL	BLISSFUL
BORED	CAUTIOUS	COLD	CONCENTRATING	CONFIDENT	CURIOUS	DEMURE
DETERMINED	DISAPPOINTED	DISAPPROVING	DISBELIEVING	DISGUSTED	DISTASTEFUL	EAVESDROPPING
ECSTATIC	ENRAGED	ENVIOUS	EXASPERATED	EXHAUSTED	FRIGHTENED	FRUSTRATED
GRIEVING	GUILTY	HAPPY	HORRIFIED	HOT	HUNGOVER	HURT
HYSTERICAL	INDIFFERENT	IDIOTIC	INNOCENT	INTERESTED	JEALOUS	JOYFUL
LOADED	LONELY	LOVESTRUCK	MEDITATIVE	MISCHIEVOUS	MISERABLE	NEGATIVE
OBSTINATE	OPTIMISTIC	PAINED	PARANOID	PERPLEXED	PRUDISH	PUZZLED
REGRETFUL	RELIEVED	SAD	SATISFIED	SHOCKED	SHEEPISH	SMUG
SURLY	SURPRISED	SUSPICIOUS	SYMPATHETIC	THOUGHTFUL	UNDECIDED	WITHDRAWN

help them find the words to express what they are feeling:

IV) It is important that the family and friends have a prepared list of specific incidents (attitudes, actions, conversations) that reveal the dysfunctional behavior. The list needs to be specific. Generalizations only allow the disease of addiction to escape; family members need to be precise about details and events. Also, it is helpful if all members keep their lists relatively short, avoiding an unnecessary overlap of incidents. Family members and friends should be prepared to share how these incidents, occasions, and actions made them feel. Intervention often has been compared to surgery, where sharp, deep, and specific incisions are made, rather than random slashings.

V) The atmosphere of the intervention should be of concerned love. It is a sequence of serious incidents that has made family and friends come together. When reading their lists, they need to look into the eyes of the religious addict and preface their remarks with a sentence like, "I really need to tell you that I love you and it is because I love you that I share the following concerns. I have observed in your religious behavior..."

VI) It is appropriate at the beginning of the intervention to ask to be heard. A specific request like, "I know this is difficult for you to hear, but please listen to what I am going to say to you. Please hear me out." This has the advantage of putting the religious addict in the role of the "listener;" he is no longer "in control."

It has been my experience that once the religious addict starts to talk, debate or argue, then the advantage is lost.

VII) It is essential to persevere with the intervention regardless of grunts, moans, shuffling in the chair or disturbing comments. Here is a dramatization of an intervention on a religious addict, loosely based upon past situations:

After having had two previous meetings preparing the wife and two daughters for an intervention on George, the religious addict, we met at their home in Los Angeles.

The first words George said when he saw me enter the room with the family was, "What is he doing here? Why have you brought a Roman Catholic priest into our home?" The eldest daughter, Marilyn, spoke up, "Dad, Father Leo is not a Roman Catholic priest. He is an Episcopal minister. And he is not here to preach religion. He is here to help all of us. As a family we need to talk about a problem that has been hurting us for many years and it is not getting any better. In fact, it is getting worse. Father Leo can help us only if we agree to be helped by him. Incidentally, Dad, if the word 'Father' offends you, and I know that it does, call him Leo."

At that point I extended my hand and said, "Hello, George. It's good to meet you. Do call me Leo." He did not accept my attempted handshake.

George replied, "It says in the Bible that you should call no man your father except God. The Bible is my guide in life and I live on the Word of the Bible. People like you are condemned by Jesus. You are today's Pharisees. Even if you are not a Roman Catholic priest, you look like one. And that is just as bad. Anyway, what do you want?''

Again, Marilyn spoke up: ''Dad, you've touched upon the problem. For years we've all suffered from your oppressive religious attitude. We love you. We care about you. But we have to talk to you and let you know how we feel because otherwise we are being dishonest to ourselves and to you.''

He immediately glared at her. Pointing his finger, he snarled, ''No daughter of mine talks about my religion. It is personal. Do you hear, Girl? It is personal. Between Jesus and me. And if you were a Christian daughter you would not talk to your father in this manner. Not in front of him.'' He made a side glance at me.

Then, in a quiet way, Maude, his wife for more than twenty years, spoke, ''George, I've never publicly disagreed with you. Or answered you back. But for once in your life, let go of your need to control this family and listen to what we are trying to share with you. Listen and be quiet. Try not to interrupt.''

''You must understand how hard it is for us to talk with you about this subject. We know how you feel about religion. But if we are going to be a family, if this family is going to heal, then we must talk about it. We have reached that point.''

For the moment, George seemed shocked into silence. It was probably the first time that Maude had ever spoken to him in such a manner.

The youngest daughter, who was seventeen and had not said a word, began to talk.

"Daddy, I love you so much. But mixed with the love is fear and hate. I am afraid of you. I'm afraid to hug you. I'm afraid to tell you I love you. And most important, you have made me afraid of God. Daddy, listening to you talk about God for all those years has made me afraid of Him."

George sat up in his chair; he was hurt and indignant. "How can you say such a thing? What an awful thing to say to your father!"

Again Maude spoke, "Please, George. Listen to what Amanda is saying. Hear her pain and then ask yourself if she is making it all up."

Amanda continued, "Daddy, I've already told Father Leo - I mean Leo - that I attempted suicide nearly two years ago. He knows I'm in therapy. I've explained that I didn't want to eat, that I'm anorexic. Daddy, I've told him more than I've told you. I've told my therapist more than I've told you. Daddy, I can't talk to you. Believe me, I'm afraid of you."

"I know you didn't mean to do this, but your view of God, religion, Jesus, the Bible, Heaven and Hell has scared me from childhood. I grew up being afraid. I know you told me that Jesus loved me, but all I ever saw and heard was hate, judgment, anger, people being sent to Hell - and I became afraid. I was afraid of God. I was afraid of you. I was afraid of my body. I was afraid of people. Daddy, I have become afraid of everything. I wanted to kill myself to avoid the fear. And yet I was scared of dying because I was afraid of Hell. And so I stopped eating. I wanted to hurt my body because it was evil. Why feed what is evil? I wanted to stop my sexual feelings by starving them. Oh, I know it doesn't make sense, but at the time, it did."

"Daddy for the last two years, we've not got along. I've lived isolated in my room. I don't pray with the family. You know I hate to go to church with you - you force me. Every Sunday, we have the same arguments. Every Sunday, we have the same threats. And I hate that church. I hate the people. I hate the pastor. And Daddy, I hate you because you have created this hate. And I feel so guilty."

"The only boyfriend I ever really liked you stopped me seeing because he was Roman Catholic. He told me to tell you he would go to our church - but still you said no. You called him an idolator. You said he worshipped statues. That he was a pagan. That he was worse than a Jew because he twisted the words of Jesus. And you stopped me seeing him."

"Years before this you kept me away from other children in the neighborhood. I had no school friends. Daddy, can you ever remember me bringing home school friends? Can you ever remember me going away to school camp? I could have no school friends. Why? Because they did not go to our church. They were heathens. They would get me into bad ways. Daddy, I hated my childhood. I cannot ever remember anything good about being a child. What a terrible thing to say! All I did was pray, read the Bible, go to school and, of course, attend church. You picked my friends. You allowed me to play with two girls from the church - and they were worse than any of the other kids in school. They talked dirty and smoked cigarettes. But because they were church kids, they were okay. Little did you know, Daddy! Oh, how I grew up hating you.

"Then the family arguments. Mother always looked silent and sad. I sensed I was developing the same fear that she had. We prayed, but we were not a happy family. If God loved us, why did He make us so unhappy? In my mind, I hated God because He was so cruel."

"I used to see other families, families that you said were going to Hell: they were laughing, playing games, talking and shopping together. As we were going to church, they were having a barbeque in the garden. How I prayed that our family could go to Hell!"

Marilyn smiled at Amanda. Amanda had said all the things that we had arranged at the pre-intervention meeting, but today, at this moment, it took on a different meaning. The hurt and emotional pain were more apparent. Amanda, for once in her conversation with her father, was being "real."

George looked stunned. Then he tried to rationalize the message he had just received. "You misunderstood me, Amanda. That Catholic boy was no good for you. I wanted only what was good for you. I wanted you to be happy."

For a few seconds we all looked at each other. He seemed helpless when confronted by his emaciated daughter. Echoing around the room were his haunting words, "I only wanted what was good for you."

Then Marilyn spoke. She was in her early twenties, but looked older. I had met her some years before at a meeting for recovering alcoholics; she had since joined Overeaters Anonymous. Now she was attempting to bring a healing message to her father.

"Dad, I was a rebel. We've learned to live with each other over the years - but we've achieved this by avoidance. I told you once before that I felt I was religiously abused in my childhood, but you wouldn't hear me. Well, when I told you that some years ago, I was speaking in anger. Today I come to you in love. Your religion - or brainwashing, as I like to call it - has nearly destroyed this family. I was into drugs at fifteen and today I know that I was escaping from my world at that time including your God. As Amanda has already said, you were a tyrant. Believe me, your God is against everything and everyone - except the chosen. Nothing was good; everything was evil. From sex, to boys, to clothes, to music; naturally alcohol, cigarettes and dancing were condemned immediately. And because your God said no to all these things, my rebelliousness said yes to it all.

"I never heard you talk about the beauty of a sunset. You never could see God in a sunset, hug, stream or loving relationship. Your God was always found in boring history, followed by judgments. It took a group of recovering alcoholics to give me a knowledge of God as I could understand Him. And I love Him. It is my knowledge of Him that gives me the confidence and power to share this message with you."

"Dad, I think you found in religion what I found in drugs. An escape from feelings. An escape from loneliness and guilt. A false courage - in your case a courage based upon being chosen and redeemed, that allowed you to feel important or needed."

"It had never occurred to me before, but I think that you and I are the same. You abused God and I abused cocaine, alcohol and food. We both hurt the people that we loved. Today, I believe you loved us, but you did not know how to show it. You hid behind the Bible. I also believe you are in as much pain as I was when you came before the judge with me and supported the probation officer's plea that I go to a chemical dependency center for treatment. Remember, you asked me to get help. I was proud, stubborn and angry - but I knew that my life was not what it was meant to be. Daddy - I've not called you that for many years - you are also proud, stubborn and angry, but I believe you are in pain. You know in your heart that the way we are living as a family is not the way it was meant to be."

"All your praying, testimonies, crusades, healing meetings didn't help me with my addiction problem. But my acceptance, surrender to the fact that I'm not perfect and that I don't have all the answers was the beginning of a new life for me. Daddy, you helped me with your support and love. Let me help you now."

Tears were running down George's face. The room was charged with emotion; that emotion was love.

Almost instinctively, George got up and hugged Marilyn. His sobs were audible to all in the room. He was not the only one crying. Amanda had also stood up and was waiting for her hug. All three formed a love-circle.

Then Maude spoke, "George, please sit down because I need to tell you something. If I don't say it now, it will never be said. George, I love you. I've always loved you. But it has not been easy. We both found Jesus at the same revival meeting many years ago. I believed that Jesus would change our lives - but never did I expect to see the change that occurred in you."

"George, today I can tell you - you became addicted

to Jesus. You became addicted to religion. You became addicted to meetings, sermons, preachers and Bible texts. Since I have attended these sessions with Father Leo, I respect his Christian tradition - even though it is not mine - and I can call him Father. I realize that I had the same feelings about your involvement with religion as a wife of an alcoholic has for her husband's use of alcohol. I felt I was being pushed out and I felt helpless.

"I silently watched the girls pull away from you. More importantly, I watched them pull away from me. Oh, sure, there were times when you made a great deal of sense, but other times you were cruel."

"I knew Amanda really liked Patrick. That spark in her eyes when she first spoke of him made me realize that at last she had found a special friend. Then you stopped her seeing him when you discovered he was Roman Catholic. And I remained silent. They were both young kids and yet you blamed him for a religion that he was born into. A thousand years of prejudice was dumped upon a young boy's shoulders."

"George, you and I need to look at our relationship. I cannot be a wife if you keep me acting and feeling inferior. You use the Bible to silence me; shut me out; to keep me feeling helpless and unworthy. At the pre-intervention meetings I realized we had three daughters - and I was one of them!"

"And yet as a wife, I know that you have a beautiful gentleness and tenderness. Perhaps today, for the first time, the girls have seen a glimpse of it. God is not evil. Religion is not to blame. The church and our faith need not be the enemy. It is how we abuse them and in turn become abused. How we twist what God has given to secure our own ends. We miss the beauty of God in our endeavors to keep laws and observances."

"George, do you remember when we first met? Long before we got married, you told me your father was dead and your mother was a little strange? We've never talked about this in front of the girls before, but this seems an appropriate time." Looking at Amanda and Marilyn, she continued, "Your grandma was an alcoholic. But she would stop drinking for months when she rediscovered religion. Remember, George? You said that the times your mother got religion were worse than the drinking times - the beatings, the screams, the accusations followed always by that punishing silence. Do you remember, George?" George nodded thoughtfully.

Maude continued, "You hated your mother's religious hypocrisy and you hated her drinking. Now, as Marilyn said, I can see the similarity."

George sighed deeply. He looked at them all and smiled. He smiled at me. In the silence of gratitude, we looked at each other. Healing had begun for us all.

Then George spoke, "Thank you. I needed to hear what you have all said. I needed to remember, Maude, my feelings as a child with my sick mother. I need to begin to look at things differently."

Then he turned and said to me, "If you can help me, Father Leo - I'm willing."

Maude interrupted. "George, we all need help. As a family, we need to learn to express our feelings. Learn how to communicate. And learn to discover God in our lives. We need to laugh again. We need treatment."

VIII) Hopefully, during the intervention process there will be some moments of reality when the religious addict sees not only the pain and dysfunction in his own life, but also the pain and dysfunction that his disease is causing others. These moments of surrender need to be followed by firm and clear directives:

"We want you to receive therapy at a treatment center for your religious addiction.

We ask you to go and get counselling."

So that the religious addict does not feel alone, or the only one with problems, the family should share their willingness and determination to be involved in the treatment and counseling. The following statement is often very helpful: "We understand that religious addiction affects family members and relationships. We know that we are affected and we want to get help. We are not just asking you to get help, we also know we need help. Regardless of what you choose to do, we have already decided to seek counseling. We ask you to come with us and get help for your religious addiction. Let us heal as a family."

The above describes an "orchestrated intervention" that for years has proved to be very successful in getting chemically dependent people into treatment; as we see, it can also be successful with religious addicts. At such interventions, those family members who have been religiously abused (co-dependents) can get in touch with how the disease has affected them and they also can get help.

There are many other interventions that take place in the life of the religious addict (or any other addict) that happen during the course of a natural day but create a *"moment."* The threat of a divorce, coming home and seeing your daughter crying, receiving a telephone call from a son who left home because he could not take any more religion, anger towards a TV evangelist, reading a self-help book, listening to music or seeing a movie that makes you appreciate the "big God" - and you realize your painful obsession. All the above can create spiritual moments (intervention) that lead to acceptance, treatment and recovery.

In my book, *Spirituality and Recovery*, I explained it this way:

> For many people, spiritual growth has come with the acceptance of a disease. The acceptance of something they cannot control in their lives. The acceptance of something that will destroy them if left untreated. The acceptance of addiction. This is the moment of a powerful and living spirituality. A. Alvariz says in his book, *The Shaping Spirit*, "There is a moment at which things come truly alive; the moment at which they are caught in all their subtlety by the imagination. They then take to themselves meaning."[4]

FOOTNOTES

1. Johnson, Vernon E., *I'll Quit Tomorrow*. (San Francisco, Harper & Row, 1980), p. 4.
2. Ibid, p. 137.
3. Yao, J.D., M.Div., Richard, *There is a Way Out*. (New York, Fundamentalists Anonymous). Statement of Purpose.
4. Booth, Fr. Leo, *Spirituality and Recovery*. (Pompano Beach, Fla., Health Communications, Inc., 1985), p. 43.

Chapter 8

TREATMENT

Religious addiction is treatable. The purpose of this book is to show the similarities between those who suffer from the disease of chemical dependency and the disease of religious addiction; and to create the awareness and stimulate discussion of religious addiction in the recovering community - and society in general. Probably more people suffer from religious addiction and religious abuse than any other specific addiction. As we have seen, there are many untreated religious addicts and religiously abused people within the recovering community, but religious addiction has never been identified as such because, until recently, nobody has ever talked about it. Religious addiction is the hidden *addiction:* the addiction that hides behind God, the Bible, and respectability!

I believe it is easier to get well than to stay sick. However, it is important that education, therapy and motivating information be provided so that people can make the necessary changes towards recovery. Miracle, it seems to me, is rediscovering that we have the God-given power as human beings to create a healthier life, a communicating family, and a better world.

Treatment for all addictions, including religious addiction, is the process of confronting this disease and monitoring the necessary changes in attitude and behavior. Treatment is the visible sign of therapy. Treatment is practically, demonstrably, systematically structuring necessary changes in our style of living; it is realizing that if the disease is progressive and observable, then so is recovery. In this sense, the disease becomes the key to treatment. If we have the courage to confront and talk about the disease, giving specific examples of how religious addiction or abuse affected our lives - rather than hiding behind vague and meaningless generalizations - then we are a long way into the treatment process. The risk is in the willingness to talk about religious addiction!

The process of treatment for the religious addict is the same as we already have in place for people suffering from other addictions described in this book. The success and interest that we are enjoying in the treatment of alcoholism and its related disorders can also be applied to religious addiction and religious abuse. We already have a "treatment program"; what we need to do is to adapt this program for religious addiction.

TREATMENT MODEL: The key is recognizing and discussing the symptoms of religious addiction because if we are able to clearly see what they are - the negative attitudes and destructive behavior patterns (dysfunction) - then the opposite lifestyle becomes the treatment goal. Let us, therefore, look again at the specific aspects of religious addiction and seek to determine an alternative approach to living:

Religious Addiction (The Disease)	*Treatment Goal*
1. Thinking in terms of black and white.	1. Being open to criticism; not always having an answer. Learning to appreciate the "gray" areas of life.

Religious Addiction (The Disease)	*Treatment Goal*
2. Obsessive praying, going to church, attending missions or crusades, talking about God or scriptures.	2. Seeking to understand the "broad" concept of spirituality; considering the "spirit" of the scriptural message. Discover God in His/Her world.
3. Neglecting world news, forgetting engagements and missing family gatherings.	3. Discovering our responsibility toward the world, God's creation: Accept responsibility for our life, family and relationships.
4. Thinking of the world and our physical bodies as evil.	4. Appreciating the spiritual "gift" - including our physical bodies. Considering the implications of the statement "God does not make junk."
5. Refuse to talk, doubt or question.	5. Spiritual growth involves doubting, questioning and discussing issues we disagree with or do not understand.
6. Sex is "dirty."	6. Appreciating the beauty of sex, intimacy and sexuality.
7. Excessive fasting and compulsive overeating.	7. Developing "balance" in our lives; moderation - particularly concerning our use of food.
8. Unrealistic financial contributions.	8. The realization that we don't need to make exces-

BREAKING THE CHAINS

Religious Addiction (The Disease)   *Treatment Goal*

sive financial payments to be loved by or accepted by God. Understanding the concept of "religious blackmail"; discussing feelings of guilt, shame, isolation and fear.

9. Excessive judgments.

9. Considering the values of tolerance, acceptance and personal forgiveness.

10. Being brainwashed and brainwashing; developing "mind-control."

10. Developing self-esteem and confidence; understanding individuality. Realize you have "permission" to express your opinions and ideas.

11. Isolation from others.

11. Needing to create atmosphere of involvement and acceptance; developing loving relationships based upon "tough love" principle.

12. Conflict with science/hospitals/schools.

12. Appreciating that God works through His/Her world. God's "spirit" of Truth is experienced through science, medicine and education. Growth comes through change.

13. Becoming physically sick (back pains, sleeplessness, headaches).

13. Healing the "whole" person: body, mind and emotions - i.e., the spiritual self.

Religious Addiction (The Disease)	*Treatment Goal*
14. Strange messages from God or angels.	14. Using common sense; being critical and objective about "strange" messages or visions. Consider their relevance to the concept of spirituality.
15. Staring - going into a trance.	15. Avoidance of induced escapes or mind manipulations.
16. Dramatic personality changes.	16. Seeking consistency and balance in the personality.
17. Unrealistic fears - the "disease cycle" of guilt, remorse and shame.	17. Learning to talk about "buried feelings" - especially concerning guilt, fear, sexual abuse and shame issues.
18. Family dysfunction, breakdown of family relationships.	18. Creating communication in family; developing relationships.
19. Geographical moves.	19. Seeking social, economic and personal stability.
20. Cries for help: physical and mental breakdown: hospitalization.	20. Stressing the need for "ongoing" recovery program; developing a support group.

Let us examine, in detail, the suggested treatment goals.

BREAKING THE CHAINS

1. *Open to criticism; not always having the answer. Learning to appreciate the "gray" areas of life.*

Slowly, we teach the religious addict and those who have been religiously abused that religion is not "black" and "white." The scriptures are inspired and the Bible records God's love for His world - but the Bible also needs to be explained and interpreted for our modern society.

Most people believed, when Saint Paul was writing his letters, that:

   (a) the world was flat,
   (b) women were inferior to men,
   (c) slavery was acceptable,
   (d) many Christian groups expected Jesus' "second coming" during their lifetime.
   (e) circumcision was an important "religious rite."

Today, because of sociological changes, political movements, science, navigation and theology, people have grown away from such beliefs. Men, women, and the church have each changed.

Nobody has the answer to suffering, persecution, famine, violence, earthquakes and so much tragedy and chaos in this world - other than to say that this is how life is, and we must learn from our mistakes. Artists, with their questions, are often more helpful than clergy with their answers! In my book, *Meditations for Compulsive People - God in the Odd*, I wrote in the chapter "Oscar Wilde":

A prophet's prophecy is rarely understood in his day,

a priest makes sacrifices with his life,
Oscar died and made men live with confusion.

Truth is rarely clear.
It often provokes fear and denial.
Truth is a double-edged sword.

When you pray to be true, beware.
When you ask for integrity, be prepared to pay.
Holiness hurts![1]

Reality requires that we appreciate and accept that we are not perfect. We live in an imperfect world; in the struggle, we discover humanity's dignity and self-esteem. The religious addict needs to see that quoting a text from scripture, for example:

"The Lord gives and the Lord taketh away;
Blessed be the name of the Lord"

is inappropriate and insensitive when addressed to a woman who has just lost her child in a car crash. Perhaps the response to such a tragedy is to hug the mother, silently support her - and then make her some soup.

2. *Seek to understand the broad concept of spirituality; consider the "spirit" of the scriptural message. Discover God in His/Her world.*

It is important for the religious addict to be presented with the concept of man being a *responsible* human being, experiencing God's gift of freedom. This involves choice. People either discover their "spirituality" and choose to be positive and creative human beings or they can stay diseased (dysfunctional), trapped with a negative attitude and a destructive life-style.

This might be an appropriate time to get the patients in group therapy to discuss the meaning of the diagram:

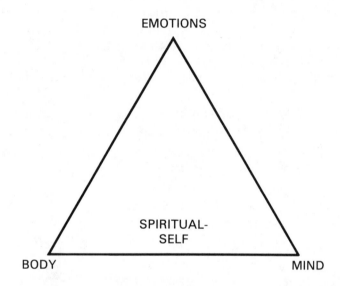

The religious addict also needs to reconsider certain scriptural texts to discover the "spirit" of the message -rather than staying with the literal text.

Jesus then said to his disciples, "I assure you: it will be very hard for rich people to enter the kingdom of heaven." (Matt. 19:23)

Happy shall he be who takes your babies and smashes them against a rock. (Psalm 137:9)

Now, to the unmarried and to the widows I say that it would be better for you to continue to live alone as I do. But if you cannot restrain your desires, go ahead and marry - it is better than to burn with passion.

For married people I have a command which is not my own but the Lord's: a wife must not leave her husband; but if she does, she must remain single or else be reconciled to her husband; and a husband must not divorce his wife. (1 Cor. 7:8-11)

Wives, submit yourselves to your husbands as to the Lord. For a husband has authority over his wife just as Christ has authority over the Church; and Christ is himself the Savior of the Church, his body. And so wives must submit themselves completely to their husbands just as the Church submits itself to Christ. (Eph. 5:22-24)

Perhaps the most important concept to present to all the patients is that God is involved in His/Her world; He is to be found in poets, artists, musicians, dancers, parents, friends *and their lives* - as well as in priests, ministers, and Old Testament prophets. We must not make God too small!

This might be an appropriate time to watch a movie like "Elmer Gantry" or "Gandhi" and discuss it in therapy group.

3. *Discover our responsibilities toward the world: God's creation. Also accept responsibility for our life, family and relationships.*

This is an appropriate time to discuss what "escape" means for the addict; especially the religious addict. How easy is it for religious addicts to transfer everything toward God and not realize their involvement with creation? How did the religious addict "use" the Bible or preacher to avoid thinking or making decisions? God is creating (or being ignored!) in the actions and decisions we make.

People, by their actions, make the word "forgiveness" understood. We make "humility" a visible reality.

Only in the lives of people can "tolerance" be understood.

Family members may find this an appropriate time to talk about "abuse" feelings:

abandonment	control
anger	shame
guilt	fear
difference	rage
loss	inferiority

4. *Appreciate the spiritual "gift" - including our physical bodies. Considering the implications of the statement: "God does not make junk."*

Let the religious addict understand that *all* human beings are spiritual - i.e., children of God. Because God made us, then something of God is in everyone of us: the image of God. Therefore, the emphasis should not be about "getting" spirituality - rather do we "discover" spirituality (the power to be positive and creative human beings; loving people) in our lives.

Many religious addicts, certainly the religiously abused, were told that they needed to "escape" from the physical world, especially their bodies, into the spiritual world. For this reason, fashion, makeup, theater, dancing, kissing, taking pride in your appearance was seen as vanity, pride and "worldliness." But the statement, "God does not make junk," enables human beings to love themselves, love their bodies, to be proud of their achievements, and cooperate with God in making a better world. In this concept we discover dignity.

Also, we can begin to discover God in His world;

plants	trees
sunsets	different cultures
other religions	variety in worship
science	medicine
music	difference
friendship	dance
birds	sex
sunlight on green grass	laughter

5. *Spiritual growth involves doubting, questioning and discussing issues we disagree with or do not understand.*

Remember, for many years, the religious addict has been told:

Do not doubt.

You must not question.

There is no discussion concerning God's Word.

BREAKING THE CHAINS

Throughout the history of mankind, indeed the history of religion (especially Christianity), there has been conflict, disagreements, schisms, "splinter groups" and persecution based upon the question, "What is Truth?"

Ayatullah Khomeini disagrees with some Shiites and other Muslim groups; Roman Catholicism, claiming to be one church, contains many factions; the "spirit" that leads so many Protestant groups has led them into a multiplicity of sects. Certainly somebody doubted, questioned or disagreed!

However, knowledge and self-improvement in all aspects of life - including religion and philosophy - can only come if one is allowed to ask questions, deliver opinions and interpretations, at times agreeing to disagree.

> Had St. Paul not disagreed with St. Peter about incorporating into the Church the uncircumcised Christians, Christianity might have remained an isolated Jewish sect!

> Copernicus disagreed with the bishops and mankind moved a step closer to scientific Truth.

> Many feminists have confronted the church about discrimination, and changes are being made: growth through conflict.

Religious addicts need to be given permission to question, doubt, and to tell others what they think rather than "what the Bible says." Or what they think it says!

6. *Appreciate the beauty of sex, intimacy and sexuality.*

Lectures and group therapy for the religious addict and the religiously abused should be directed toward developing a healthy attitude towards sex, understanding and accepting our "humanness" as it relates to our sexuality - seeing sex as an expression of God's gift of love and intimacy.

Again, an emphasis on the statement, "God does not make junk." Our physical bodies, our sexual organs, menstruation, sexual intercourse - as an expression of a responsible love and affection or culminating in the birth of a child - are all aspects of spirituality.

In my book, *Say 'Yes' To Life - Daily Meditations*, I wrote:

> Sex is most beautiful because it enables the human being to experience and give love at an intimate and personal level. It also combines all the spiritual senses of body, mind and feeling in one expression, balancing tenderness with strength, patience with desire, need with selflessness.
>
> Also, the awareness and experience of a beautiful sexuality should be taken into all other manifestations of life - work, leisure, friendship, sports and prayer.
>
> The gift of sex is one of our finest and most creative attributes and leads to all that is noble in man; therefore, it should not be used irresponsibly.[2]

7. *Develop balance in our lives: moderation - particularly in our use of food.*

The religious addict needs to begin to understand the dynamics of obsessive and compulsive behavior; recognizing that people can abuse alcohol, drugs, food - and also God, scripture and Jesus. And it is people who are being abused!

Religious addicts need to see how they have created powerlessness and unmanageability in their lives; see how they missed the love of God by developing a craving for rules, absolutes, judgments and perfection. The religious addict needs to understand and accept that confusion is part of what it is to be human, that nobody has all the answers, that God is revealing Himself/Herself in many varied and different ways (consider the different world religions and various Christian denominations) - therefore tolerance and moderation is essential for the spiritual life.

8. *Don't need to make excessive financial payments to be loved or accepted by God. Understand concept of "religious blackmail"; discuss feelings of guilt, shame, isolation, and fear.*

Many religious addicts will talk about the excessive financial payments they made during their religious addiction. They need to express how these excessive payments affected their lives, their families, their relationships. Many will have feelings of anger, guilt, fear and rage!

Remember, most were blackmailed into giving:

If you give . . . . you will be forgiven.

. . . . your child will be healed.

. . . . your sickness and pain will go away.

. . . . all your problems will disappear.

. . . . peace will come to your family.

.... the starving will be fed.

.... more will be given to you.

.... you will be reunited with loved ones in heaven.

Many group members will have been religiously abused by this excessive tithing - not having enough food to eat, clothes to wear, books to read, games to play; and for years, they blamed God. I wonder how many children of religious addicts have anger, rage, and hatred toward God - and have grown up with this buried anger?

9. *Consider the values of tolerance and personal forgiveness.*

Many recovering addicts in Twelve-Step programs are familiar with the phrase, "Go with the flow"; the world is created in wonderful difference and we will exhaust ourselves trying to make it the same. We need to accept the imperfection of ourselves, others and the world and stop trying to make it (and them) the way we want it to be!

The fourth and fifth steps of the Twelve-Step program might be helpful for religious addicts - getting them to see how the disease affected their lives and begin to journey towards personal forgiveness.

Step 4: "Made a searching and fearless moral inventory of ourselves."

Step 5: "Admitted to God, to ourselves and to another human being the exact nature of our wrongs."

BREAKING THE CHAINS

Only when people are willing to confront their dysfunctional behavior, recognizing how it affected their lives and the lives of others, is *personal forgiveness* possible. Hiding the problem, not willing to recognize the destructive attitudes, hoping it has gone away - only continues the denial process, keeping us sick.

10. *Developing self-esteem and confidence; understanding individuality. Realize you have "permission" to express you opinions and ideas.*

Religious addicts need to change the old tapes that emphasized bad, dirty, sinful, unredeemed, lost, and begin to explore and develop a positive and creative understanding of themselves. Then they can begin to appreciate the dynamic concept of spirituality.

God has blessed us with a brain. It is not a sin to think. We are thinking people. It is okay to express opinions and make suggestions. God's revelation is a process, not an event! God works through His/Her people.

The religious addict needs to consider the idea of humility involving self-respect, a healthy pride and confidence to express personal beliefs. The specialness of being a child of God needs to shine in our assertiveness.

11. *Need to create atmosphere of involvement and acceptance; developing loving relationships based upon "tough love" principle.*

Many religious addicts and religiously abused, especially the women, have felt isolated, discounted, shut out, abandoned and inferior - and they need to talk about these feelings. Also they need to be part of a developing program (similar to Alcoholics Anonymous, Overeaters Anonymous, Adult Children of Alcoholics, which are local, national and, eventually, world-wide) - a self-help program that is started in treatment and continues with a progressive recovery plan based upon self-help groups.

Therapy work concerning self-acceptance and group acceptance will be important in getting the general public to realize that religious addiction/religious abuse is a disease, a compulsive and obsessive behavior that is similar to the other addictions currently being treated at chemical dependency centers. The general public needs to understand that religious addiction really does create, as we have seen clearly demonstrated in the pages of this book, abusive behavior that affects all relationships, creating chaos, needless suffering and pain. The clause within the American Bill of Rights that guarantees freedom of religion does not protect the right of any individual, in the name of God or any religious creed, to abuse the lives and intellectual freedom of others. White supremacists, whose religious creeds encourage the persecution of blacks and Jews, are not at liberty to abuse the well-being of other citizens. In a similar way, the general public needs to understand that the religious addict is not protected by the American Bill of Rights to abuse, in the name of God, his family or those who do not share his religious beliefs. As with the many aspects of co-dependent behavior, the religious addict and those affected by religious addiction could be helped by the techniques developed at many chemical dependency centers.

An advantage of having the religious addict involved in treatment with other addicts is that they will be confronted in group (tough love) and they would also learn to identify with the other addicts - growing in a therapy of self-disclosure and self-discovery. Developing a loving relationship with "self" and family members would be an appropriate function of this treatment program - recognizing how God, the Bible, and ministers were abused and abusers in their past dysfunctional life-styles.

12. *Appreciate that God works through His/Her world. God's "spirit" of Truth experienced in science, medicine, and education: Growth through change.*

Again, an emphasis on the fact that it is God's world; He created and *is* creating through His world.

It is important for the religious addict to consider the achievements and discoveries that have been made and are being made because of man's varied endeavors. Science, medicine and education are not the enemy of God or the Bible - rather, they are to be seen as important aspects of spirituality. Man's enemy is ignorance, superstition and closed-mindedness.

In treatment, the religious addict and other group members should discuss this - sharing any personal stories and incidents that reveal religious dysfunction.

13. *Healing the "whole" person: body, mind and emotions - the spiritual self.*

The religious addicts need to recognize how their

dysfunctional attitudes and behaviors have affected every aspect of their lives. As with alcoholism, it is a "cunning, baffling, and powerful disease" and it affects the whole person.

The counselor or therapist should lead the group in a discussion of the following diagram.

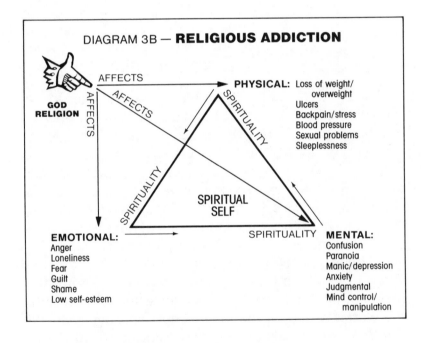

DIAGRAM 3B — **RELIGIOUS ADDICTION**

14. Use of common sense; being critical and objective about strange messages or visions. Consider their relevance to the concept of spirituality.

BREAKING THE CHAINS

For many years the religious addict had a belief system that was told to him by a minister, a priest, parent or TV evangelist. He was told:

This is what God said...
This is what God did...
This is what God expects...
This is what God will do...and you must
not doubt.

This is what happened in the Bible...
This is what the prophets declared...
This is what God condemns...and
you must not question or
doubt.

However, if we take the Bible as an example, it is a book that contains a variety of writings: history, poetry, autobiography, stories, parables, allegories and documented opinions. They also were written at various stages of man's development, under different conditions and situations, in many cultures, in response to a variety of political systems, by different writers - having many backgrounds, with a multitude of purposes and intentions, different styles of writing and vocabulary. To simply describe all these historical manuscripts as "the Word of God" and not seek to explain or interpret the mind or method of the writer is a gross injustice to God, the writer/writers of the manuscripts and the listeners! Common sense tells us we should not do this. Indeed, the history of the Christian church tells us that we should not do this because, for political or theological reasons, in the early church some books were acceptable for a time and then they were thrown out. As an example, the Book of Revelations, for a period of time, was considered a gnostic writing and was not included in the New Testament. Then the church decided to include it.

There are many people who are in psychiatric hospitals and have declared that God, Jesus, or Mary gave them a message for the world. But strange messages and visions cannot be uncritically accepted. Again, common sense is required. Therefore, when a preacher like Oral Roberts says:

"I've had to stop a sermon, go back and raise a dead person," adding good-naturedly, "It did improve my altar call that night."[3]

without verification, or "reasonable accountability," then the critical concept of common sense needs to be applied.

15. *Avoid induced escapes or mind manipulations.*

The religious addict needs to avoid any pressures or experiences that create "escape." The religious addict in treatment needs to accept and learn how to live with reality. Freedom to think, doubt, share opinions and offer criticism is the goal for the religious addict - mindful that he should be open to receive what he puts out!

It might be useful to examine the religious addict's use of alcohol, drugs (including prescription drugs) and food. As we have seen in earlier chapters, religious addicts may abuse other drugs or have co-dependent behavior that is creating powerlessness and unmanageability in their lives, alongside their religious addiction. Also, they should be given information concerning the nature of cross-addiction, warning them of the dangers of chemical dependency once they stop their religiously addictive behavior.

This is another reason for the religious addict and religiously abused to have a self-help support group.

16. *Seek consistency and balance in their personality.*

The religious addict has been experiencing "highs" caused by prayer meetings, crusades, sermons, feelings of being the chosen or the redeemed, healing services, chants and other ecstatic "religious experiences" - followed, usually, by bouts of depression, sinfulness, fear, loneliness and confusion. It is important that the characteristic of "balance" be presented in treatment.

This balance and consistency is possible when religious addicts understand that they are loved by God, that God has accepted them as they are - therefore, they must seek to love and accept others. A healing personality can only develop in knowing that we are healed through God's love - not through judgment!

17. *Begin to talk about "buried feelings" - especially concerning guilt, fear, sexual abuse, and shame issues.*

Religious addicts probably became compulsive and obsessive concerning religion because they did not feel "good enough." Often they were the children of parents who were religious addicts - and the disease had been passed on. Some have been sexually abused; all have been emotionally abused and therefore, the hurt and pain needs to be expressed.

In the meditation, "My Name is Shame," I discussed some of these buried feelings:

I came upon you - when you were young.
When you were very young:
  before you understood,
    before you could speak,
      before you realized I was there.

I came upon you.

I created feelings of unworthiness,
          disgust,
            inferiority,
             ugliness,
              stupidity,
               poverty,
                and difference.
  I tarnished the image of God.

I existed before the guilt.
  I lived before the action.
    I was the whisper before the sound.

Always, I enter through the back door,
        unseen,
        unwanted,
          the first to arrive.

Guilt grows in me.
    Guilt finds its strength alongside me.
      I mold guilt into shape:
      My name is Shame.

The World asks, "Where does Shame come from?"
      From anywhere and everywhere.
The condescending glance from a parent.
    The awkward appearance in the mirror.

> The cruel remark from children.
> Feelings and actions condemned by the
> preacher.
> The touch that does not feel right.

I come from anywhere and everywhere![4]

18. *Create communication in the family; develop re-lationships. As we have seen, religious addiction affects the family.*

It is important in treatment that family members and significant relationships are involved. The religiously addicted parent needs to hear how the disease has affected the spouse, children, friends and employees.

The issues of co-dependency should be explained to family members and the adult children need to see how it is affecting their lives and relationships. The counselor or therapist must appreciate that the same denial that is seen in the family members of other addicts is also evident in religious addiction. Lectures, group therapy and private sessions should be arranged with family members and significant relationships.

Family members also need to be open to looking at chemical dependency issues (i.e. eating disorders) in their own lives. What have they "used" to coexist with a religious addict? How did they bury their feelings? What dysfunction has it created in their lives? (See Chapter 3 - The Family)

19. *Seek social, economic and personal stability.*

The religious addict and family members (co-dependents) need to create and be introduced to a self-help support system that will help them continue their recovery after treatment.

In treatment the religious addicts have been examining the powerlessness and unmanageability created by an abuse of religion (God); however, in recovery, they should expect to create and sustain a "power" and "manageability" that reveals itself in forgiveness, self-esteem, acceptance, joy in living, tolerance, concept of an inclusive God, freedom to think, doubt and ask questions - self-love.

The religious addict has had a "spiritual awakening" and this will include the social, economic and personal stability he is creating in his world.

20. *Emphasize need for "ongoing" recovery program; develop a support group.*

Twelve-step recovering alcoholics and addicts say that they are not cured; their compulsive and obsessive behavior is arrested - a day at a time. They are recovering. In a similar way, the religious addict needs to develop an ongoing awareness so that he never forgets:

what it was like,

what happened,

what it is like now.

The history of all compulsive people (regardless of drug or behavior) has been that once they forget, ignore their past, stuff their feelings - it all comes back! They may not always go back to their original drug (obsession) but they create a similar dysfunction in their lives;

they recreate a new "victim role." I believe this is also true for the religious addict.

The treatment staff should assist in developing a supportive self-help program at the hospital or in the community - including a self-help support group for the co-dependent family members. (See the suggested Twelve-Step program at the end of this chapter.)

Mindful of the information that has been recorded in this book, I believe that it would be relatively easy to absorb the religious addict and religiously abused person (and family) into the existing chemical dependency treatment center. Indeed, I would suggest that most treatment centers already include patients who are religiously addicted - but nobody has specifically defined it or developed a "treatment track" to treat it. Most of the personal stories and incidents that have been mentioned in previous chapters have come from my experience at various chemical dependency treatment centers. However, there comes a time (and I believe the time is now) when a specific obsessive and compulsive disease needs to be named and treated - although the symptoms have been around for centuries. Religious addiction needs to be brought out of the closet!

As an inpatient or outpatient at a chemical dependency treatment center, or attending therapy groups for compulsive and obsessive disorders, the religious addicts should seek to turn their dysfunction in a new and different direction. The dysfunctional religious attitudes have not been working for them - now is the time to look in a new direction. The "detox" concept might be helpful for the religious addicts in that they need to get away and have an inpatient stay in a chemical dependency center so that they can concentrate on how the disease of religious addiction has affected their lives and relationships. Once religious addicts start to recognize their compulsive disorder, discuss specific instances of how their religious addiction developed and manifested itself (see Religious Addiction Progression chart - p. 63) then, hopefully, they will begin to initiate significant changes in behavior and attitude.

Religious addiction needs to be treated as a specific addiction, alongside other obsessive and compulsive disorders, with a consistent treatment plan worked out by a therapist or counselor to ensure a thorough and comprehensive recovery program. God only knows (literally) how many millions of people suffering from religious addiction or religious abuse have never found their way into therapy and have suffered and died isolated in their disease.

Treatment Program:

Would a religious addict - or those who have been religiously abused - benefit from other treatment components found at a chemical dependency treatment center, or would they need to be on a completely separate and distinct track? I think the religious addicts would benefit from being involved in the complete program - having a few separate therapy sessions or "one-on-one" sessions specifically concerned with their religious addiction or abuse. But the greater part of any chemical dependency treatment program would contain pertinent information for any religious addict. And the identification that would take place with alcoholics, co-dependents, and adult children of alcoholics in the group would be especially relevant. Remember, many religious addicts are children of alcoholics or come from dysfunctional homes. Many have a rampant or controlled eating disorder. A great number of religious addicts were sexually abused or have a hidden sexual addiction. The issues of co-dependency, therapy work concerning self-esteem, creating healthy relationships and discovering "the child within" would be particularly helpful. The value of having a religious addict attend groups would be in creating the awareness of yet another hidden addiction!

Many of the chemically dependent patients would be able to identify with the incidents and buried feelings of the religious addict. Indeed, religious addiction would become the focus of a relapse discussion: people believing that God would keep them sober.

Other aspects of treatment that would be helpful for the religious addict/religiously abused person to attend:

Lectures. Topics relating to addiction and compulsive behavior:

> Medical aspects of addictive behavior
> Psychological aspects of addictive behavior
> Family rules and family roles
> Changing lifestyles in recovery
> Increasing self-esteem
> Adult children of dysfunctional families
> Co-dependents in treatment - Why?
> Relapse

Naturally, we would now include a lecture on religious addiction and religious abuse!

Educational Films: As with the lectures, it would be good for the religious addict to see films that might include:

Alcoholism and the Family
The Enablers
Soft is the Heart of a Child
It Will Never Happen to Me
The Dry Drunk Syndrome
I'll Quit Tomorrow

Perhaps the treatment center would also include films like:

Elmer Gantry (Burt Lancaster)
Power and the Glory (Gregory Peck)
Agnes of God (Jane Fonda)
Rise of Islam: Islamic Fundamentalism
Jonestown Tragedy
Sex information films.

Nutritional/Exercise Information:

It is important for religious addicts and those who have been religiously abused to take care of their physical bodies.
Discussion concerning healthy eating.
Sexuality and good nutrition/sleep.

BREAKING THE CHAINS

Spirituality Group:

The day should start with a spirituality group that is based upon a love and acceptance of self. Also a love and acceptance of others - especially those who come from different cultures and religions, or none. Mindful of the fact that some patients would be agnostic or atheist!
Meditation exercises: Based upon "neutral" concepts;

love	sexuality	music
nature	joy	humor
hugs	honesty	sobriety
variety	forgiveness	tolerance
animals	food	power

Family Treatment:

The religious addict has affected his/her family. It is important for family members or significant relationships to be involved in treatment. Remember, many of the parents of the religious addict will also be religious addicts; and the religious addict's children will be religiously abused.

Issues for the family include;

denial	powerlessness
detachment	obsessiveness
low self-esteem	trust
expression of feelings	tolerance
communication with others	sexual dysfunction

Based upon Janet Woititz' list, issues for the adult children of the religious addict will include:

Adult children guess at what normal is.

Adult children have trouble following a project through to the end.

Adult children lie when it would be just as easy to tell the truth.

Adult children judge themselves without mercy.

Adult children have difficulty having fun.

Adult children take themselves very seriously.

Adult children have difficulty with intimate relationships.

Adult children overreact to changes over which they have no control.

Adult children usually feel different from other people.

Adult children are super-responsible or super-irresponsible.

Adult children are extremely loyal, even in the face of evidence that the loyalty is undeserved.

Adult children tend to lock themselves into a course of action without giving serious consideration to alternative behavior or possible consequences.

Support Groups:

It will be especially helpful if the religious addict and religiously abused attend outside Twelve-Step support groups with other patients, attending, whenever possible, some Fundamentalist Anonymous meetings. The religious addict might, early on in treatment, begin to identify with the personal stories and feelings of other addicts; he/she will no longer feel alone, separate and different.

Fundamentalists Anonymous considers the Twelve

Steps of Alcoholics Anonymous to be potentially harmful for the religious addict and religiously abused because of the emphasis upon a Higher Power and God. They consider that it would awaken a destructive identification with past religious practices and that references to God or Higher Power could create a relapse syndrome - taking the person back to a harmful identification with religion. *However, I do not agree.* If the Twelve Steps are seen to be the basis of a spiritual program and not a religious organization, then the religious addict is not only able to be incorporated completely into a developed support group system but also has before him a world-wide recovery fellowship, creating self-esteem and a positive attitude toward life.

Twelve Steps for the Alcoholic:	*Suggested Twelve-Step program for religious addicts:*
1. We admitted we were powerless over alcohol - that our lives had become unmanageable.	We admitted we were powerless over religion - that our lives had become unmanageable.
2. Came to believe that a Power greater than ourselves could restore us to sanity.	Came to believe that a Power greater than ourselves could restore us to sanity.
3. Made a decision to turn our will and our lives over to the care of God *as we understood Him.*	Made a decision to turn our will and our lives over to *the care of God as we understood Him.*
4. Made a searching and fearless moral inventory of ourselves.	Made a searching and fearless moral inventory of ourselves.
5. Admitted to God, to ourselves, and to another human being the exact nature of our wrongs.	Admitted to God, to ourselves and to another human being the exact nature of our wrongs.

6. Were entirely ready to have God remove all these defects of character.

Were entirely ready to have God remove all these defects of character.

7. Humbly asked Him to remove our shortcomings.

Humbly asked Him to remove our shortcomings.

8. Made a list of all persons we had harmed and became willing to make amends to them all.

Made a list of all persons we had harmed and became willing to make amends to them all.

9. Made direct amends to such people wherever possible except when to do so would injure them or others.

Made direct amends to such people wherever possible except when to do so would injure them or others.

10. Continued to take personal inventory and when we were wrong, promptly admitted it.

Continued to take personal inventory and when we were wrong, promptly admitted it.

11. Sought through prayer and meditation to improve our conscious contact with God *as we understood Him,* praying only for knowledge of His will for us and the power to carry that out.

Sought through prayer and meditation to improve our conscious contact with God *as we understood Him,* praying only for knowledge of His will for us and the power to carry that out.

12. Having had a spiritual awakening as the result of these steps, we tried to carry this message to others, and to practice these principles in all our affairs.

Having had a spiritual awakening as the result of these steps, we tried to carry this message to others, and to practice these principles in all our affairs.

The Twelve-Step program would be helpful because:

The Twelve-Step program is the most successful self-help support system for compulsive and obsessive people in the world.

The Twelve-Step program is specifically a spiritual program, incorporating people and cultures from every part of the world, and is not allied with any religion or denomination. Indeed many atheists and agnostics belong to Twelve-Step programs.

The Twelve-Step program speaks to the essential nature of an obsessive and compulsive (addiction) disease - incorporating family members (co-dependency) and adult children.

The Twelve-Step program develops and encourages a positive and creative approach to God "as you understand Him"; teaching us to be responsible for our lives and relationships.

Many people who are already involved with a Twelve-Step program for a specific addiction (i.e., Overeaters Anonymous) will be able to utilize the same program for religious addiction or religious abuse.

The Twelve-Step program is already in existence and is progressively (one day at a time) developing recovery and healing for millions of people suffering from addiction and co-dependency. Why reinvent the wheel?

The Twelve-Step program proclaims a positive message based upon personal responsibility (the miracle within) rather than seeking a magical solution (dysfunctional religion). This is an important message for the religious addict.

The Twelve-Step program speaks of a "spiritual awakening," a discovery of God (Love) within us. This becomes a powerful message to other suffering addicts, perhaps eventually healing the world.

FOOTNOTES

1. Booth, Fr. Leo, *Meditations for Compulsive People - God in the Odd*. (Pompano Beach, Fla., Health Communications, Inc., 1987) p. 29.
2. Booth, Fr. Leo, *Say Yes to Life - Daily Meditations For Recovery*. (Pompano Beach, Fla., Health Communications, Inc., 1987) p. 27.
3. Ostling, Richard N. "Raising Eyebrows and the Dead." *Time* Vol. 130, (July 13, 1987) p. 55.
4. Booth, Fr. Leo, *Meditations for Compulsive People - God in the Odd*. (Pompano Beach, Fla., Health Communications, Inc., 1987) p. 138-9.

Chapter 9

RECOVERY: SAYING "YES" TO LIFE

In Alice Walker's book, *The Color Purple*, we observe how Celie changes and grows as a human being, discovering her spiritual specialness that is above and beyond any religion, allowing her to be a woman. With Shug, Celie learns about the "Big-God":

She say, My first step from the old white man was trees. Then air. Then birds. Then other people. But one day when I was sitting quiet and feeling like a motherless child, which I was, it come to me: that feeling of being part of everything, not separate at all. I knew that if I cut a tree, my arm would bleed. And I laughed and I cried and I run all around the house. I knew just what I was. In fact, when it happen, you can't miss it. It sort of like you know what, she say, grinning and rubbing high up on my thigh.

Shug! I say.

Oh, she say. God love all them feelings. That's some of the best stuff God did. And when you know God loves 'em you enjoys 'em alot more. You can just relax, go with everything that's going, and praise God by liking what you like.

God don't think it dirty? I ast.

Naw, she say. God made it. Listen. God love everything you love - and a mess of stuff you don't. But more than anything else, God love admiration.

You saying God vain? I ast.

Naw, she say. Not vain, just wanting to share a good thing. I think it pisses God off if you walk by the color purple in a field and somewhere and don't notice it.

What it do when it pissed off? I ast.

Oh, it make something else. People think pleasing God is all God care about. But any fool living in the world can see it always trying to please us back.

Yeah? I say.

Yeah, she say. It always making little surprises and springing them on us when us least expect.

You mean it want to be loved, just like the Bible say.

Yes, Celie, she say. Everything want to be loved. Us sing and dance, make faces and give flower bouquets, trying to be loved. You ever notice that trees do everything to git attention we do, except walk?[1]

We are now beginning to see the light at the end of the tunnel. Recovery is possible for the religious addict and those who have been religiously abused only when they begin to appreciate the concept of the "Big-God": discovering God within the happenings of ordinary life, realizing that God is involved in the everyday choices we make. Recovery for the religious addict is discovering divinity in our own lives.

God is understood as the Creator: We need also understand that God is creating - and He/She is especially creating in and through our lives. We are co-creators with God. We are not puppets on a string waiting for "something to happen." We make things happen. We create the difference. In our determined choice, the miracle exists. This is our "yes" to God. Alan Ecclestone explains it this way:

The Yes to God means something more. There is the right response that all creation could be said to yearn to make, the creaturely desire, however buried and distorted it may be at times, to be itself, to be the work of God, which with a fine audacity the writer of Genesis will describe as being 'very good.' Right faith in God expects it to be so expressed. 'Sing, O ye heavens; for the Lord hath done it: shout, ye lower parts of the earth; break forth into singing ye mountains, O forest, and every tree therein; for the Lord hath redeemed Jacob, and glorified himself in Israel.' This is the Yes that every man and woman, inside and outside churches, inside other faiths or none at all, will by striving to be human, express in some degree in unremembered acts or in self-giving with a dedicated life. Its roots are in compassion, appreciation, delight, and tenderness and love. Its growth is manifest in works of mercy, healing, education, justice, social welfare, respect for things and creatures of every kind. Its flowering is in art and science, in marriage, parental love and all commitment to delighted patient use of human powers.[2]

This contrasts sharply with the attitude of so many religious addicts and those who have been religiously abused. For them, God is specifically seen outside the created order - distant, detached, judgmental, aloof, removed, separate from His creatures. God is seen as coming from the outside to judge, condemn, destroy, and separate. Because the religious addict and those who have been religiously abused have difficulty appreciating or seeing God in their lives, they become dependent upon a particular "Go-Between." It is the Go-Between who interprets, explains, tells you what God expects, gives direction, decides what is right or wrong. The Go-Between tells you what God is like -making the religious addict a victim of his own belief system.

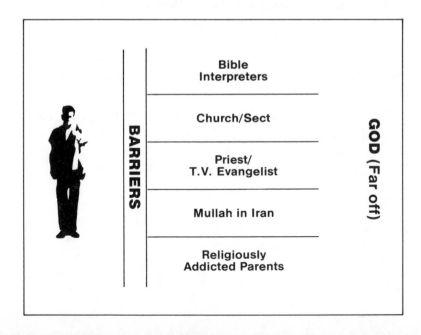

And eventually you become what you believe; the God you experience is reflected in your behavior and attitude.

The religious addict feels controlled - and so he learns to control.

The religious addict feels judged - and so he learns to judge.

The religious addict feels dirty and sinful - and so he makes others feel dirty and sinful. And so it goes on.

The religious addict will remain a victim so long as he believes that the "power" exists outside himself; so long as he misses the gift of spirituality in his own life. Recovery, not only for the religious addict, but also for the alcoholic, the addict and the other compulsive people, is realizing that we have "the power" to create a healthier life,

healthier relationships,

a healthier world.

Because God is involved in our lives so also is His Power. In recovery we appreciate that we are powerful human beings.

What does spirituality mean? It is related to the word "spirit" and instead of imagining a white-sheeted ghost flying in and out of our lives (i.e., a child's concept of the Holy Ghost), we should emphasize:

Energy
Creative Choice
A powerful force for living.

When we say, "This horse has spirit," or, "The spirit of the nation was rekindled," we mean that a positive and creative energy is realized, witnessed or perceived. The power to live, work, create is actualized. In a similar way, a spiritual person is a positive and creative human being. They know, deep inside of themselves, that they make the difference. They have located their "yes" to life.

In *Spirituality and Recovery*, I explain it this way:

The kind word can only be said if we choose to say it. That needed word of encouragement or forgiveness requires *you*. Others may say it, but that would not be you. It would not be you saying it. Remember, nobody can say it like you. You are terrific.

In your individuality is your uniqueness.

In your individuality is your power.

In your individuality is your divinity.

Everything stems from how you choose to practice your Spirituality. The word of encouragement or the silence of understanding.

All are part of life.

All are our responsibility.

Even the negative and critical statements are ours.

We choose to hurt.

We choose to be cruel.

We choose to destroy.

BREAKING THE CHAINS

The awareness of our imperfections can be the way back to our given Spirituality.[3]

Returning to the diagram of the human being that we have used in earlier chapters - spirituality affects the *whole* person.

EMOTION

GOD

SPIRITUAL POWER

PHYSICAL   MENTAL

The God within us does not make junk! Therefore, the whole person - physical, mental, and emotional - is infused with divinity.

PHYSICAL: God is alive in our bodies - therefore, He exists in sexuality, intimacy, childbearing, hugs, exercise, nutrition - - all are aspects of spirituality.

MENTAL: God is alive in our minds - therefore, doubting, asking questions, criticism, appreciating artists, changing attitudes and beliefs are all part of the spiritual growth.

EMOTIONS (Feelings): God is alive in our emotions - spiritual growth includes talking about feeling abused, discounted, abandoned, judged, sinful, inferior, angry, or lonely.

Dr. Martin Israel, in his book, *Precious Living*, says:

The very distinction between spiritual and material or sacred and secular, is ultimately invalid, for the spiritual mode finds its place in all actions, whether physical or psychical, that lead us to a fuller knowledge of God. Whatever leads us to a knowledge of God is spiritually based; it also leads us away from preoccupation with ourselves to a fuller participation in the world's affairs and the concerns of other people. All this is summarized by Jesus' two great commandments: "Thou shalt love the Lord thy God with all thy heart, and with all thy soul, and with all thy mind, and with all thy strength. This is the first commandment. And the second is like it, namely this: Thou shalt love thy neighbor as thyself" (Mark 12:30-31). The beauty of nature, the marvelous rhythm of the cosmic flow, and the processes of our own healthy bodies are all fundamentally physical in scale, and yet are also deeply spiritual in content, for they lead the beholder to rejoice in God the creator and sustainer of the universe. Great art, again sensual and physical in its outer manifestation, is humanity's finest spiritual creation, for it leads the weary soul to its Creator Who is the end of all beauty. Likewise the scientist dedicated to the pursuit of truth is God-centered and spiritually based, for in God is all truth. Those whose lives are devoted to service and care for others are equally spiritual in orientation, for they tread the path of self-giving service in love, and God is above all else love. From this we can deduce that physical communication has strong spiritual overtones when it is inspired by the highest values we know - beauty, truth, and goodness (or love).[4]

We do not "get" spirituality, it has already been given. Recovery for the religious addict will be in discovering their God-given spirituality, the power that will enable them to realize their freedom.

The first step of the Twelve-Step program for A.A.

states: "We admitted we were powerless over alcohol and our lives had become unmanageable."

So long as the alcoholic is using alcohol (or any other mind-altering chemical), his life will reveal a powerlessness (helplessness) and an unmanageability (irresponsibility) that will progress into despair and death. Recovery begins when the alcoholic "sees" what is happening (intervention) and begins to make changes in lifestyle and attitude.

In a similar way, this is true for the religious addict. "We admitted we were powerless over religion and our lives had become unmanageable."

The religious addicts need to "see" that their pain, family problems, discomfort, loneliness, low self-esteem, guilt, shame and isolation are the result of their powerlessness concerning religion; their religious cravings have resulted in unmanageability. When the religious addict begins to understand that God is not a prisoner of any religion, T.V. evangelist, sect, guru, or church, then he can become open to accepting the creative concepts of spirituality, experiencing a "power" and "manageability" in his life.

Let us again examine the "recovery" section of the religious addiction chart:

RECOVERY FROM RELIGIOUS ADDICTION

Life gets better
& better.

Confidence in family/friends
Have peace of mind

Appreciation of
spiritual values.

Rationalization recognized.
First steps towards economic stability.

Begin contentment in freedom
and self-acceptance.

Increase of emotional control.

Increased interest in therapy.

Adjustment of family need.

Appreciation of real values.

New circle of friends.

Rebirth of ideas.
New interests develop.

New set of moral values begin unfolding.

Face future courageously.

Natural rest and sleep.

Decrease of escape anxieties.

Diminishing fears and anxieties.

Self-esteem returns.

Application of spiritual values.

Family/friends appreciate efforts.

Belief that new life is possible.

Begin realistic thinking.

Regular nourishment taken.

Dawn of new hope.

Spiritual needs examined.

Attempts at honest thinking.

Begin listening to others consider
God's uses in the world.

Told religious addiction can be
arrested.

Begin to grow in group therapy.

Desire for religion persists.

Attempts to stop religious addiction.
Learn religious addiction is a disease.

Express desire for help.

Meet normal, happy, recovering spiritual people
in Fundamentalists Anonymous.

Hospitalization (for
nerves, emotional
breakdown)

BEGIN RECOVERY
(Calls for Help)

BREAKING THE CHAINS

We have seen that religious addiction, like all addictions, all obsessive and compulsive behaviors, produces a negative and destructive lifestyle. Therefore, recovery is seen in turning the disease (the dysfunctional behavior) in a new direction, thus developing a positive and creative attitude. It sounds too easy! I believe it is easier to get well than to stay sick; it is easier to go with the flow than to fight and discount ourselves and others; it is easier (and more fun) to experience God in our lives than to hide from Him in fear and shame.

Dr. Martin Israel says:

Joy comes from within; it is assuredly present in the world, but it does not come to us merely from agreeable outer circumstances. Rather it is the radiant joy from within ourselves, the knowledge of God immanent in our own being, that sheds radiance on the world, raising it from the corruption of mortality to the splendor of eternity. Joy came to me whenever I could center my attention, in child-like wonder, on any phenomenon or object. As I have said, I knew, early in my life, the joy of identification with nature in her many forms: the countryside with its changing pattern of beauty, from spring blossoms to the yellow summer grassland, the flowers of the field, the autumn tints of brown and red, and the sharp cleansing winter barrenness when all was desolate and yet full of that true beauty that comes of a shriven landscape. In nature there is not merely the outer form, but also an inner realm that palpitates with psychic and spiritual life. To him who can observe there is nothing empty save the emptiness of a vapid, selfish human being intent only on himself and his needs.[5]

Religious addiction and religious abuse have created a dark prison, a barrenness, walls of fear that prevent risk, creativity and spontaneity. Recovery will come when we understand that we have the power to break the chains, to experience real freedom in our shouted "yes" to life.

Recovery reflects our yes to God and also our yes to self. Recovery appreciates with gratitude the gift of being allowed to be co-creators with God. We begin to comprehend that God speaks and works through His creation, and this involves you and me. We are not spectators; we are creative participants!

We understand the Truth that God is in us, and therefore, the values that we attribute to Him/Her should also be realized in our lives. The qualities that we use to describe "the God of our understanding" should also be experienced in us.

GOD/values	*SPIRITUALITY/*(Recovery)
1. *Truth/Honesty*	1. *Truth/Honesty:* We seek to be honest in our lives and relationships, realizing that our journey toward Truth is the key to self-awareness and self-worth. Integrity comes with "walking the talk."
2. *Freedom*	2. *Freedom:* Religious addiction made us slaves, living in fear, loneliness, anger and isolation. Our goal in recovery is to experience the freedom to think, ask questions, criticize and explore the intellectual world. In recovery, we have the freedom to explore our own individuality; we have the freedom of choice.

3. *Forgiveness*

3. *Forgiveness:* The forgiveness that we attribute to God we should also afford ourselves and others. The mistakes and failures that we realize in our lives should help us understand the failures and mistakes of others. True identification leads to forgiveness. Only in understanding forgiveness will we experience freedom.

4. *Energy*

4. *Energy:* God creates through us. Rarely do miracles just happen. They require our involvement: lepers walked, blind people shouted, prophets preached and poets created music with their choice of words. Perhaps the greatest gift the human being has received from God is energy. We are still creating this universe.

5. *Love*

5. *Love:* We reflect God's Love in the way that we love ourselves and others. God requires our love to sustain the world. But this love must be based upon creative truth, hence the value of art in

man's quest for a realistic spirituality. Alan Ecclestone suggests:

Before ever a Yes to God can be made, the creature must come alive to the moment and the circumstances and the implications that have to be faced. What poetry does is to awaken a man or woman to the moment, to shape the preparedness from which the response can be made. Spirituality is not simply a widening of the consciousness as some enthusiasts for drug-cultures have suggested, or an increasing of the sensitiveness of human beings, but the employment of all that we have of sensitive awareness and rich consciousness in acts of faithful living. The prayer that we make is the focusing of that effort. What poets can do, and what we need them to do, is help us to be more adequately prepared in the persons we are for that engagement of ourselves with God.[6]

6. *Joy*

6. *Joy:* A deep and vital joy is perceived in knowing that we are children of God and that our creative power is endless. But more than this, it is okay to have fun in our lives. We reflect our gratitude to God in being able to play in His garden.

7. *Peace*

7. *Peace:* We begin to understand that things get better (peace) when we seek in our lives the values we attribute to God. The journey into God becomes a journey into self; and in discovering who we are, we experience a God of our understanding. Peace comes with the awareness of a God with whom we can live and play.

8. *Acceptance*

8. *Acceptance:* What God has created, He also accepts. In the acceptance of creation is Love. We need also accept ourselves and others because only then will we be able to create. Spiritual acceptance comes when we discover something of ourselves in others - and in the universe.

9. *Variety*

9. *Variety:* God had created the world in variety and He is perceived through "the many." Truth is a many-sided diamond. Obviously, for the Christian, God has especially revealed Himself in Jesus - but God is alive and real in the other great religions and phi-

losophies of the world. Alan Ecclestone comments:

> No more appalling image of Christ's Passion in the world has been presented to us than that continued age-long persecution of the Jews in Christian Europe. Failing to honor the distinctiveness of Jewry, the Christian Church has weakened its own power of learning what it means to the people of God in a hostile or indifferent world. It has failed again and again to live out the implications of an Exodus theology, and to be warned by the facts of the Exile.[7]

10. *Humility*

10. *Humility:* The root meaning of humility means ''of the earth''; the humble person understands that he is not exalted above others - but he is not beneath others! The humble person has a true estimate of self-worth; a healthy ego. Humility resists forcing people into thinking only what you think. Also humility will not be intimidated. Humble people carry the strength of knowing that they are a child of God - with power.

11. *Humor*

11. *Humor:* There is a saying, ''If God created you, me and

monkeys - then He must have a sense of humor.''

Humor allows us to bring a perspective to our lives; it stops us from taking ourselves too seriously. We realize we are not God and we can let go of the control. The world will still be there in the morning! Many religious addicts were taught that humor (fun) was sinful. That laughter was an offense toward God because it refused to treat the world seriously. Nothing could be further from the truth. Humor allows people to heal. Humor appreciates the joy in life and relationships; it understands the creative aspect of "playfulness," allowing for relaxation and family nurturing.

12. *Change*

12. *Change:* To live is to change. Because almost daily, we are learning new things about the universe, relationships and ourselves, it is important that we remain open, flexible and tolerant of "new ideas." The religious addict claims to have the answer - only to discover

that the vast majority of people are asking different questions!

Jesus said, "When, however, the Spirit comes, who reveals the truth about God, he will lead you into all the truth" (John 16:13). The implication of these words is that we will be on a journey, discovering new and different values along the way. The inability to change stops the journey into God; stops our "yes" to life. Arnold Wesker's comment is pertinent: "So then, he'd say: 'Bridges! bridges! bridges! Use your bridges, woman. It took thousands of years to build them, use them!" (Roots)

So recovery for the religious addict is experiencing the need to say "yes" to life. Not having all the answers, sometimes feeling alone and afraid, being confused and angry at the pain and suffering in the world — yet aware of moments when God's Love is alive, real and special in our lives. We have seen that the religious addict escapes life by rules, regulations, laws, judgments, dogmas and a dysfunctional separateness. The recovering religious addict shouts a "yes" to life in all of its perplexity.

For the spiritual person, the end is always the beginning of the journey. The "not knowing" becomes the focal point of a creative energy as experienced in scripture, song, music, dance, poetry, and in *one person sharing his story with another person who has been there!*

****

Abandon yourself to God as you understand God. Admit your faults to Him and your fellows. Clear away the wreckage of your past. Give freely of what you find and join us. We shall be with you in the fellowship of the spirit, and you will surely meet some of us as you trudge the Road of Happy Destiny.

May God bless you and keep you - until then. (Alcoholics Anonymous: A Vision for You)

FOOTNOTES

1. Walker, Alice, *The Color Purple*. (New York, New York, Simon and Schuster, 1982) p. 203-204.
2. Ecclestone, Alan, *Yes to God*. (London, Darton, Longman & Todd, 1976) p. 2-3.
3. Booth, Fr. Leo, *Spirituality and Recovery - Walking on Water*. (Pompano Beach, Fla., Health Communications, Inc., 1985) p. 39.
4. Israel, Martin, *Precarious Living*. (London, Hodder & Stoughton, 1976) p. 95.
5. Ibid, p. 23.
6. Ecclestone, Alan, *Yes to God*. (London, Darton, Longman & Todd, 1976) p. 58.
7. Ibid, p. 18.

AFTERWORD

I am concerned that those suffering from religious addiction and abuse receive the same professional help and support as any other addict. It is my intention to develop a family treatment program for religious addiction and religious abuse. Perhaps some of you who have been religiously addicted and religiously abused would care to write about your experiences explaining what happened to you, and how you got help and the support you are receiving today. If you give me permission to write about your experiences, it may help others.

For further information, write:

> Emmaus Limited
> 195 Claremont Ave., Suite 388
> Long Beach, CA 90803
> (213) 434-4813

Together let us break the chains!

Support Group for Religious Abuse

Fundamentalists Anonymous
P. O. Box 20224
Greeley Square Station
New York, New York, 10001

ABOUT FATHER LEO

Father Leo Booth is an internationally known spiritual educator and lecturer. He is a native of England and was educated at King's College and St. Augustine's, Canterbury. For a short time he tutored the Chaplain's course at Christ College, Cambridge, on the subject of "Spirituality and Addiction." He is a certified alcoholism counselor and certified eating disorders counselor.

Father Leo had a personal "moment" in 1977, following an automobile accident, when he recognized that he was an alcoholic. Following treatment at Warlingham Park Hospital in Sussex, England, he began to devote his energies to helping other alcoholics and their families by his own methods of recognizing the "give-ness" of spirituality. He defines spirituality as: "that which enables the development of creative and positive attitudes in all areas of life." He believes that spirituality is not an interesting option for the addict; it is an essential component in recovery.

Father Leo speaks at conferences, universities and hospitals around the world. As a spiritual consultant on addiction, he lectures, conducts spirituality groups and is involved in the clinical treatment of hospitalized chemically dependent patients. Father Leo implements his ideas of spirituality in recovery from religious addiction, co-dependency, sex addiction and other compulsive behaviors. He utilizes spirituality (not religion) in the dynamics of recovery, which has proved an essential ingredient to "self-love" and the exercise of "personal power."

Father Leo has appeared on "The Oprah Winfrey

Show," "The Today Show," "Hour Magazine" and "USA Today," as well as numerous radio programs, to discuss aspects of spirituality and recovery. He is a contributing editor to *Professional Counselor Magazine,* which serves the alcohol and drug addiction field. He has his own television show, "Say Yes to Life?" a weekly series of programs dealing with addictions and the recovery process.

Other Books by Father Leo

Say Yes to Life... Daily Meditations

Meditations for Compulsive People

Spirituality and Recovery... A Guide to Positive Living

Videotape

Father Leo has developed a lecture concerning religious addiction and abuse—available on VHS.

Audiocassette

Father Leo describes the symptoms and effects of religious addiction on a cassette entitled "Recovering from Religious Addiction and Religious Abuse."

For more information on both the videotape and audiocassette, write to:

Emmaus Limited
195 Claremont Avenue
Long Beach, CA 90803
(213) 434-4813